Building Your Career Capital

How to create value and stay ahead in the talent race

Nitin Thakur & Peter Freeth

Genius Media
CREATING KNOWLEDGE

2023

Building Your Career Capital

Nitin Thakur & Peter Freeth

ISBN 978-1-908293-40-4
First Edition September 2023

Genius Media 2023

Published by:

Genius Media
B1502
PO Box 15113
Birmingham
B2 2NJ

geniusmedia.pub
books@geniusmedia.pub

Contents

Talent

Leaders all over the world are talking about the 'war for talent'. They tell us about the need for organisations to build succession plans and develop the leaders of tomorrow, and they invest in leadership and talent programs to develop a 'talent pool' to make sure that a lifetime of valuable business knowledge isn't lost at a critical moment.

Until the 1990s when many large organisations underwent radical restructuring thanks to 'Business Process Re-engineering', many people could count on a job for life. 'Baby boomers', born through the 1940s, 1950s and early 1960s, tended to stay longer with their employers, and expected loyalty in return but during the 1990s, when entire layers of middle managers were stripped out, the 'Generation X' workforce thrived on a diet of performance related pay, individual appraisals and a greater focus on productivity over time spent in the office.

Where this leaves us today is that for the past 30 years, you have not had the full time management support structure behind you that previous working generations enjoyed, planning your career path and taking care of your daily needs. Your manager has his or her own targets and objectives, and HR probably have to chase managers to perform annual appraisals. Many companies are getting rid of appraisals because they 'don't work', however it may be more likely that it's simply too much trouble to get line managers to spend the time doing them, and the result of 'ticking the boxes' is that they're ineffective.

In short, no-one is taking care of your career, you have to do that for yourself.

During the past 30 years, organisations have sought to create ever more efficient processes and systems. We have seen the introduction of lean manufacturing, Six Sigma and Enterprise Resource Planning, made possible by the internet which became an intrinsic component of almost every part of a global business.

In the 21st century, the focus is changing. With the fabric of a business running on automated systems, the human factor once again becomes the critical differentiator in achieving not only business success, but in this economic climate, survival.

The graduate and talent programs of major corporations are designed to predict who has the potential for progression and then to develop that potential in order to build a solid 'talent pipeline' or 'talent pool' of people who are ready for promotion.

Employers know that employees might have plans to develop their careers elsewhere, so they have more high potentials than there are senior positions. Employees know that there are not enough positions available, so they keep their options open for external positions. It's a vicious circle which can lead to a lack of faith in the talent program from both sides.

The root cause of the problem is that talent programs are notoriously ineffective at predicting actual future performance, and if you think about it, the reason is obvious. How can you reliably predict your ability to do something that you have never done before?

The assessment centres, reviews and action learning projects of talent programs are an attempt to predict the future, but they will never provide the same challenge as a real promotion, with the ongoing day to day pressures of a senior position.

The inaccuracy of these predictions makes business leaders and HR professionals 'hedge their bets' with more candidates than roles, and in return, the candidates hedge their bets by considering other options. Inefficiency leads to waste, which means that your talent program is costing more than it should.

How, then, can you both improve the accuracy of these predictions and ensure that your own potential is accurately predicted?

In this book, we will explore these two perspectives. Improving the accuracy of your predictions is valuable for hiring managers and recruiters, whilst ensuring that your own potential is recognised is valuable for anyone.

More than this, there are two central paradoxes to your development as a 'high potential'.

The first is very obvious, yet is overlooked by almost everyone involved in talent management. The word 'potential' means:

- Adjective: having or showing the capacity to develop into something in the future.

- Noun: latent qualities or abilities that may be developed and lead to future success or usefulness.

By its very definition, your potential comprises anything that you haven't done yet. How can you measure or predict your future actions and strengths?

If you plant a seed in your garden, how do you know what it will grow into? How tall will it be? Will it produce flowers or fruit? Will the fruit be edible or poisonous? You can't know until it is fully grown. You might think that you know what species it belongs to, so you know to expect roses or strawberries. That's like saying that you're a member of Homo Sapiens so you'll grow up to be an investment banker. What will *this specific* plant grow into? We have to wait and see.

The second is that you cannot hire yourself, so your challenge is not to develop your own skills and experience, but to focus on what those skills and experience mean to the person who is hiring you. What you think of yourself is irrelevant. Feedback about how you are perceived is everything; it is your brand, your personality, your place in the world.

In this book, we will address and resolve both of these paradoxes, and you will learn everything that you need in order to be recognised as not only a high potential candidate but *the* right candidate, the *perfect* candidate.

The Risk of the Unknown

Stock market analysts make a career of predicting the future, and usually their actual performance is no better than if they picked stocks at random. In an experiment conducted by the British psychologist Richard Wiseman in 2001, three investors were given £5,000 of imaginary money to invest in the FTSE 250 stock market. After one week, the performance of the three was compared to see who had made the best predictions; a financial analyst, a financial astrologer or a four year old child picking stocks at random.

The financial analyst said that he was targeting stocks he felt were "oversold and likely to have a short-term bounce".

The financial astrologer said, "Because there is an angle between Jupiter and Neptune which might favour technical stocks, I'll move over towards those stocks".

The four year old child said, "I'm going to make my mummy a fortune by picking the winners".

At the end of the experiment, the analyst had lost 7% of his capital, the astrologer had lost 10% and the child had lost 4.5%. Critics said that comparing performance over such a short period of time is an unrealistic test, so the stocks were compared again a year later. This time, the analyst had lost 46.2% of his capital, the astrologer had lost 6.2% and the child had gained 5.8%.

You have no doubt heard the phrase, "past performance is not an indicator of future results", yet as humans we do indeed expect change to continue in the same direction. Our minds are adept at seeking and creating patterns in the world, and even ancient civilisations built huge solar calendars to predict the changes of the seasons. The problem is that physical cycles can follow a predictable pattern because of underlying physical rules, however there are no such rules governing the behaviour of other people. Whilst you have habits and preferences, it's impossible to predict what you'll do next year based on what you achieved this year.

If you just bought a flight ticket, there's a good chance you'll travel in the near future. If you just bought a thick winter coat, you're probably travelling somewhere cold. Retailers use such data to push targeted advertising at you, based on the probability that if you buy certain products, you'll need some complimentary products too. Do you want an apple pie with that?

This type of prediction is based on 'big data', or data collected from large numbers of transactions. Whilst this might be helpful in predicting how many people will add an apple pie to their order, we can't have any confidence in saying *which* customers will follow that prediction.

In workforce planning, knowing that your turnover of staff in a customer service call centre is 40% is all you need. That prediction enables you to scale your recruitment and training activities to maintain the right workforce. Once you get to senior management levels, the picture changes. Knowing that you'll lose 20% of your executives this year isn't helpful, you need to know which ones are moving on because succession planning for specific business functions now becomes the priority.

Therefore, by the time an employee reaches the level of authority where talent management becomes relevant, we want to know who will perform in the next role and who won't, and this driver has created a huge industry for psychometric tools which promise to reveal the secrets of the candidate's mind and enable you to predict their future performance with great accuracy.

These claims are, of course, ridiculous. The kinds of character traits which are tested using psychometric tools have little bearing on a person's behaviour because a person does not work in isolation; their character adapts to the environment around them and is influenced by the other people in that environment.

However, talent assessment is big business; worth around $9bn in 2022 and so the companies that provide these assessments have a vested interest in exploiting your human tendency to believe in patterns and predictions. Add to this your tendency for

The Risk of the Unknown

confirmation bias, and you'll remember the times that the prediction was right and conveniently forget the rest. In fact, you'll read the personality description of your 'type' and find it amazingly accurate, but you won't read all the others to see if they're accurate too. Similarly, people will read the description for their astrological star sign or Chinese horoscope sign and be amazed at how accurate it is, but generally won't read the other eleven. Try it, and see what you find.

What you might summarise from all of this is that it's impossible to predict what an individual person will be able to do in the future. The counsellors and self-help experts would take the view that everyone is capable of anything, yet most experienced managers will always remember that candidate who seemed so capable in the interview and then utterly failed to deliver once hired. The hiring manager will of course blame the candidate or the agency for this. They will rarely blame their own recruitment methods, and they will usually fail to take into account the importance of the alignment between the candidate and the organisational culture.

The conclusion that we have reached and which we hope will address all of these issues is simple.

You cannot predict potential.

You can only measure performance.

Recruiters are most concerned about potential when someone is making a significant step change in the challenge of a role. The greater the step up in challenge, the greater the need for the hiring manager to be certain that the decision will be right. If you're hiring a delivery driver, you can make a decision based on their references and interview performance and, if they don't work out after a week, you can let them go and no significant harm will have been done. When you're hiring a new CEO, the risk of failure is far higher and recruiters agonise for months over their decision. It's likely that they're not focusing on making the right choice, they're focusing on making a safe or defensible choice, just in case things go wrong.

What everyone is trying to do is reduce risk.

Imagine that you are standing at the bottom of a cliff, looking up. How do you plan to climb up it? You might:

- Look for an easier but longer route

- Look for obvious steps such as boulders or flat areas

- Use climbing equipment

- Make a detailed plan

- Give up

Assessing and reducing risk is a natural function of your mind. You do it automatically when you plan a journey, cross the road, try a new restaurant or apply for a job.

You intuitively know how to assess and reduce risk because your mind is built for predicting the future. However, predicting the likely trajectory of a football that's heading your way is very different to predicting how a new restaurant or new management recruit will turn out.

In the distant past, ancient tribes relied upon their wise men, seers, soothsayers, scryers, witch doctors and clairvoyants to predict the future. Will the crops fail? Will the sun come up tomorrow? Will we survive the winter? Today, our society is still dominated by soothsayers, only today we call them stock market analysts, sports commentators and 'futurologists'. And of course, astrology is still big business.

Most importantly for this discussion, you will tend to predict trends where non exist. If you're a hiring manager, you'll use a candidate's account of their past performance to predict their potential. If you're a candidate, you respond by talking about your career history as if there was a strategy which led to a string of successes and achievements when the reality is more likely to be a series of carefully covered-up disasters, political wranglings and missed opportunities. The history books are written by the victors.

One executive search consultant told us that he is looking for candidates who demonstrate a "career trajectory", a series of 'dots' that he can join up to estimate a person's potential. He's not looking for proven experience, because that would limit the number of potential candidates, so he tries to minimise the risk of the hiring recommendation by seeking candidates who have a track record that implies they are heading in the right direction. In the world of head hunters, every search consultant knows every candidate. What no-one knows is a potential candidate. By looking at career trajectory, he is trying to predict who will be a high performer in the future, while the regular recruiters are fighting over the candidates who have already proven themselves. This also reveals an interesting point that we will return to later, that your current performance is the result of your past actions. What the search consultant is looking for is future results arising from today's actions.

In reality, the search consultant is not looking for a prediction. He is looking for a plausible story that he can sell to his client.

Confirmation bias is a feature in our thought processes which makes us seek evidence for the things that we already believe to be true and which also makes us ignore evidence that suggests we might be wrong. In the headhunter's case, he would never try placing a random candidate, just to see if his 'career trajectory' theory is valid. He believes that he always 'gets it right' because that is the basis on which he sells his services to corporate clients, and he can explain his methodology in great detail. He can't take the risk of trying something different because it might fail and spoil his success story.

A famous international rugby player told us that he starts preparing for a game the day before he leaves home. He packs his bag in the same way each time and even eats the same meal. Logically, this can't have any connection to the way that he plays, but in his mind this is a routine which he can't change for fear of affecting his performance. Confirmation bias reminds him of the times that his routine was disturbed, resulting in failure. It also deletes from his memory the times that he followed his ritual and lost. His approach is not scientific, but he would strongly defend that it "works for him" and, since it doesn't harm anyone, why change what works? His routine has no intrinsic benefit, but it does influence his state of mind, his focus and therefore his playing ability. If he's physically unfit on the morning of a game, it's too late to do anything, but if he's in the wrong place mentally, he can adapt and self-correct much more quickly.

Recruiters have their own rituals, including their own interviewing style and choice of psychometric tools. They don't really know if these 'work' or not, but they can't deviate from their routine for fear of getting it wrong.

One more example of cognitive bias which will cause problems in the assessment process; the Dunning-Kruger effect. In 1995, a man named McArthur Wheeler robbed two banks in Pittsburgh. He learned that invisible ink can be made from lemon juice and then covered his face in lemon juice, believing it would make him invisible to the CCTV cameras. David Dunning and Justin Kruger at Cornell University read about this, and wondered how the bank robber could have been so stupid. What they discovered is that unskilled people tend to over-estimate their own capabilities, whereas highly-skilled people tend to under-estimate their capabilities.

The Dunning-Kruger effect is "a cognitive bias in which relatively unskilled persons suffer illusory superiority, mistakenly assessing their ability to be much higher than it really is. Dunning and Kruger attributed this bias to a metacognitive inability of the unskilled to recognize their own ineptitude and evaluate their own ability accurately. Their research also suggests corollaries: highly skilled individuals may underestimate their relative competence and may erroneously assume that tasks which are easy for them are also easy for others." (Wikipedia)

There is an argument to be made for the courage of naivety, the willingness to throw yourself into a new venture without care for the potential for failure. People who avoid pushing their boundaries for fear of it going wrong might be described as over-cautious, risk-averse, afraid of failure. Knowledge is relative and you simply don't know what you don't know. Armed with a little knowledge, McArthur Wheeler might well have thought that if lemon juice can make itself invisible then maybe it can make other things invisible too. However, a moment's critical analysis would reveal that whilst the juice made itself invisible, it did not make the paper invisible.

The same process of extrapolating a little knowledge leads to many of the opinions which you will see shared on social media. The Earth looks flat therefore it is. Getting to the Moon seems complicated therefore the Moon landings were faked. Australia doesn't exist because it would break the 'flat Earth' theory. Birds don't exist, they are government spy drones. The COVID vaccine was a government control system. 5G mobile is a government control system. A pattern of thinking seems to underpin such ideas.

Our minds are simulators, sensory processing systems which enable us to learn complex rules and predict the future, creating an illusion that we are in control of our choices rather than simply reacting to external events. We take a few observations and from them, extrapolate a scenario which we can then either embrace or avoid. We use this rule-making ability to jump to conclusions about people we've just met, on the basis that they remind us of other people. Hence, you are never impartial when it comes to your assessments of other people. You jump to conclusions based on the way they dress and the way they talk, and as a result of this you can buy countless books telling you how to dress and act during an interview. You can even be told the psychological impact of different colours that you might choose to wear. If we really made up our minds about people based on a neutral analysis of the facts, such books and beliefs would not exist.

Putting all of this together, we arrive at a critical point. As a candidate wishing to demonstrate your potential, you over-estimate your strengths and forget any examples of your own failings. On the other hand, the hiring manager thinks that they know everything about you from a handful of casual observations, and they will extrapolate those observations into their assessment of what you can do in the future, indeed what you will do.

Your challenge, then, is to overcome your own biases, whilst exploiting the biases of others.

Let's assume that, in terms of your intelligence, capability, experience and knowledge, you are distinctly average. Let's assume that you are equally as capable of doing a particular job as anyone else might be. There might be minor variations between candidates, and when all other things are equal, the hiring manager will amplify those differences so that they become critical decision factors. Your goal, as a candidate, is always to display those differences in a way which makes it easy for the hiring manager to notice them. Your challenge is that you don't know which differences are important to the person making the hiring decision.

As a candidate, you cannot assume that all recruiters and hiring managers are applying the same objective criteria. In fact, you have to assume that their decisions are entirely subjective and that the playing field is far from level. The only way to navigate the various barriers and obstacles is to understand what each decision maker is looking for, and the problem there is that they don't want to tell you, because they want to be the person making what they believe is an objective decision. In short, they

The Risk of the Unknown

don't want to be sold to, they want to feel in control, which is all part of their ritual.

Hiring managers will use their HR managers and external recruiters for the same reason; to reduce the risk of the hiring decision. If you don't have the data to make a safe decision, you'll use a tool to do it for you (like a calculator) or you'll ask someone who you perceive as a trusted expert. When recruiters sell their services to corporations, these are the two elements that they aim to establish in the client's mind – their expertise, and their trustworthiness. Everyone is standing at the bottom of a cliff, looking up with no idea of how to reach the top safely.

If we bring the cliff metaphor back to the hiring decision, a hiring manager will reduce the risk by trying to predict the candidate's potential using various methods which might include:

- Use external experts to make the decision

- Use trusted tools to make the decision

- Get personal recommendations from trusted contacts

- Impose a probationary period on new hires

- Take high performers from competitors

- Prefer internal candidates

Whilst all of these methods make the decision 'easier' for the hiring manager, they present barriers for the candidate. If a hiring manager only works with one retained recruiter and that recruiter has a strong bias against the company that you currently work for, you're in a very weak position. There's not much that you can do about that, other than to keep looking. You might try to make direct contact with the hiring manager, but the agency will probably have already told their client to push all enquiries back to them.

Selling yourself is no different to selling anything else. Most people picture a good salesperson as someone locked in a tough negotiation with a customer, perhaps using their skills of influence to overcome objections. In fact, the best sales people spend hardly any time negotiating and 'closing deals'. Most of their time is spent filtering out the prospective customers or 'prospects' who they're wasting their time with, a process known as 'qualification'. The best sales people concentrate their efforts on the prospects who demonstrate the greatest likelihood of success. Your search for the next step in your career isn't spent in interviews, giving slick, well-rehearsed answers to clichéd questions, it's in your ability to deal quickly with rejection, perform thorough research and target yourself precisely to roles which are the closest match to the capabilities and qualities which you can easily and quickly demonstrate to a decision maker.

Building Your Career Capital

The term "human capital" has been around for a long time, as a different way to say human resources, recognising that people are assets to a business, and that a business relies on people for competitive and strategic advantage. That's a view based on people doing the jobs that they are in, but that creates a conflict. You're not reading this because you're interested in the job that you're doing today; you're interested in the job that you will be doing next year or in ten years time, or perhaps you might plan on running your own business one day. To do anything in the future you need to invest in order to create a path to get you from where you are to where you want to be, and the funding for that path is your career capital.

A business needs money to operate. Why? Because the world needs money to work. In order to sell things you have to buy them first, or at least buy the raw materials. The fundamental purpose of any business is to make money, to create a profit. That is why we call it a business and not a charity or a social venture. Those organisations do exist, and they can be just as complex as any business but their purpose isn't to make money. The purpose of a business is very clear; to make profit by adding value. You need money to buy raw materials, pay people, develop new products, and so on. A business spends money on these things and at some later time, customers will pay money for whatever product or service the business creates. There is always a delay in a business between having to spend money in order to develop people and products, and customers paying money for the product or service that they consume. The business needs capital upfront and then cashflow every day.

A publicly listed business raises capital through share offerings. You sell some shares, shareholders give you money, you have some cash and you can go and spend that on whatever you need.

What kind of things does a business spend cash on? Product development, people, offices, lawyers, cars, expensive holidays for sales people. But the problem is that now that those shareholders have bought a piece of the business they have an influence and their influence tends to be only about one thing which is profit. The only reason they've invested in you is to make money. It's an investment, they could put money in the bank, they could make a loan to a friend to buy a house, they could visit a casino, they could invest in countless ways so they always want some return for their money. They put some money in, they take a risk, they want to get more money out, and because they want to get money out they exert an influence on the business, and that influence can be seen in the organisational culture, through the activities which are measured and rewarded.

How does the shareholder influence affect you on a day to day basis? Ideally, the shareholders want all the profits but they also know that if they take all the profits there's nothing left to invest in the business and so the business fails through lack of investment, so the shareholders know that they can't take all of the profits.

There are some things a business can do to increase share value which makes the company seem more valuable due to the price of the share stock. What kind of things can a company do to increase its share value?

- Buy other companies to increase its size

- Form partnerships and alliances to increase capability

- Develop market leading new products and IP

- Develop exclusive new technologies

- Announce large sales contracts

- Make promises about future growth

If you look at annual reports of companies, they will have chairman's statements at the start which are not just about "We made lots of money this year" it's also about "We did something for the environment", "We had some input into education", "We took care of our people" and these are all important because investors and shareholders know that those are the kinds of activities which give a company long term health, and that allows the company to survive short term financial problems or changes in the external market environment.

Everyone knows that the stock market will crash from time to time because inflated share prices are based on perception and expectation and, every so often, those expectations grow faster than the real cash revenue of the businesses. Something happens which affects the market's confidence, such as the collapse of the 'sub-prime' housing finance market in 2008 which led to a global recession. The amount of money in everybody's bank account didn't change, but money is simply an idea, a shared agreement. When the value of that idea changed, the resulting panic destroyed trust in the value of money.

We know that markets will slow down and speed up and we can't control that, but if the people within the business are in good health it's easier to survive those times. Similarly, you have events that happen in your life that create stress but if you're in generally good health you'll cope with them. If you're not taking care of yourself, if you're not getting enough exercise, if you're not getting enough sleep then one-off stressful events affect you much more.

Company shares vary in value and value is subjective. Company shares don't have intrinsic value, they have a perceived value based on future expectation. A shareholder can only sell a share for what it's worth to someone else. Share price is usually affected by financial results, so every quarter a company might announce sales results, and that might increase the share price.

Why would it do that? Simply, because it gives shareholders confidence about the future. Results are always a reflection of what you did in the past. Your sales figures this quarter are a reflection of what you did six months ago or a year ago. By the time you look at the results it's too late to change them, you already did the things that led to those results. Do you remember the imaginary seed that you planted earlier? By the time you see rose buds developing, it's too late to grow strawberries.

What the results do is to imply that you will carry on doing certain things and if you deliver what you promise or predict, you will build confidence or trust. If you have hit a sales target five times in a row the expectation is that you will continue to do that. If you produce prize-winning roses every year, most people will presume that your winning streak will continue.

Human beings are obsessed with predicting the future even though we're really bad at it because the future doesn't exist. We create the future through our actions today. We think that we're really good at predicting future results because our brains are evolved to predict the future based on our recognition of past patterns, so when we think we spot a pattern we will commit to it. This is what happens in the mind of a compulsive gambler. They think they have worked out the secret, they know that there is a pattern to the roulette wheel or the cards and they think they have a higher chance of being successful than anyone else. Of course the house always wins. In the case of the share price of companies, who is the house that always wins? Whether the share price goes up or down, the market always makes its commission.

Value is subjective and it is based on what you did in the past. The human beings who make the market will assume that what you did in the past will continue, and that then becomes the future which builds confidence or trust. When the level of confidence is high, investors will invest more money because they believe they can beat the system, because they believe they can get a return that's better than the market. Investment fund managers compare themselves to the market average. Everyone is trying to beat the system.

At the beginning of this book, we mentioned an experiment in which three people made selections from the London stock market to compare their performance.

At the end of the week-long experiment, the analyst had lost 7% of his capital, the astrologer had lost 10% and the child had lost 4.5%. Critics said that comparing performance over such a short time is an unrealistic test, so the stocks were compared again a year later. This time, the analyst had lost 46.2% of his capital, the astrologer had lost 6.2% and the child had gained 5.8%.

A business can't maintain the same strategy over long periods of time. Even if you do nothing, even if you carry on doing the same things every day, someone else is doing something different and your customer's expectations are different. Regardless of the business you're in, your customer's expectations have changed because of retailers like Amazon. New features such as same day delivery, money back guarantees with no questions asked or free delivery all change the consumer's perception of 'customer service'. The people who are your customers are also customers of Amazon and they are getting same day or next day delivery on millions of items in stock, and that level of service is affecting the consumer's expectations of every supplier.

What this leaves us is a gap between today and tomorrow.

Today   Tomorrow

We don't know what is in the gap. We don't know how to get over the gap and that's where all the problems lie with organisational change programs and corporate strategies. We're trying to predict and control the future by doing the same things that we did yesterday.

We sit here today, we make a strategy, we make a plan. We think we know what the future will look like or what we want it to look like and we're going to make a plan for how we get there and that strategy creates change. By definition, doing something different creates change.

Change needs money because you have to do things that you're not doing today. You can't simply stop spending money in one place and spend it in another. It takes time to change. If you want to innovate, you have to be prepared to give up your old ideas.

If your business makes tables and you decide to switch to making chairs, you need time and therefore money to produce new designs, buy new equipment and materials, retrain your staff and change your marketing activities. Meanwhile, your customers are still buying – and expecting – tables.

If you are currently employed and you want to start your own business, you need capital to invest because your salary will disappear as soon as you resign, but income from your new venture will take time to develop.

Many people in this situation say that they'll run their business in their spare time and when they're making enough money they'll resign from their 'day job'. Unfortunately, if you work in your day job for 40 hours a week and sleep for 56 hours a week, that leaves 72 hours a week for eating, your family, shopping and all of the other things that you have to fit in. The reality is that you do not have any spare time, every minute of every day is fully occupied. There is not one moment of your life where you are sitting around, doing nothing. Even when you think you're doing nothing, you're resting and recovering for the next day.

Building Your Career Capital

There simply isn't enough time available to generate the level of income that your day job pays you, and that's the investment gap which leaves so many people feeling trapped in a corporate job. The solution could be a bank loan, or if you're lucky, a redundancy payment. The solution could also be that you run your own business during corporate office hours and hope that no-one notices how little 'real' work you're doing.

This also applies to a situation where you need to study and gain a qualification in order to support a promotion or career change. In reality, you can't study in your spare time because you don't have any spare time. The only way to make time is to prioritise, to sacrifice something else that you're already doing. The simplest way to do this is to realise that your study *is* your job, and to make time for it during your working week. If you think you're too busy to make your studies your priority then you will never make the changes you want, because in order to create change you first have to create space.

Change creates risk because no matter how much planning we do, we never know if it's going to work out how we expected. We feel confident because we think we're clever and we've spotted a pattern, we think we can beat the system, but there is always a huge risk. What does risk create? Conflict. As soon as you get multiple people involved in strategy development they all have different ideas about what the risk means, how to manage it, how to reduce it and how to get across the gap as safely as possible. This conflict is caused by fear.

If you've ever been to a corporate event or training course and you've tried to get a group of colleagues to decide where to go for dinner, you will know that even the most simple decisions become impossible once more than two people are involved.

What we're trying to do is move from the security of today. The security of knowing where we are, knowing what works. We know that if we do certain things, if we sell these products and if we have these customers we know what to do. We know how the system works, we feel safe. We also know that our security today is always under threat. For example every existing customer of yours represents new business for your competitors. Many companies pay their sales people an incentive for finding new business, so that creates a bigger threat than if everybody is just protecting their existing accounts. The insurance and mobile phone industries are entirely based on getting customers to change supplier every year.

Although we feel safe and secure in our comfort of today, we also know that because of change in the market and technological innovation and the activities of our competitors, we're standing on an island, and that island is shrinking.

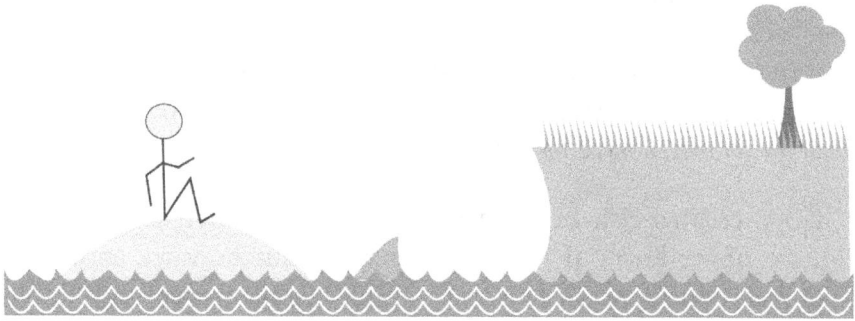

We know that if we don't move then the island will soon be gone and we'll drown, but every day we've got to negotiate that gap, and every day, the gap seems to get a little wider.

We need to create change and change is scary. Because the future is unpredictable, we minimise that risk by formulating a strategy.

Having a strategy means that you're making a guess about the future. It can't be a perfect guess, but you hope it's better than reacting to changing circumstances. You may not reach the exact destination you had in mind, but it's better to have a sense of your own direction rather than to drift.

As soon as you create a strategy, you create conflict.

You can't stay where you are, because you are standing on an island that is continually shrinking, because the market is moving, your customers' expectations are changing, and your competitors are innovating and evolving. Staying where you are means you're going backwards.

As soon as you make a plan to move, you introduce uncertainty. When people are in an uncertain, unpredictable environment, they feel unsafe and insecure. Everyone might agree that moving is the best option, but how to move, and when, and to where?

Everyone might agree on the necessity for action, but individual fear of failure means they disagree on the best course of action. If this conflict cannot be managed effectively, the result will be indecision, inaction and, ultimately, failure.

You choose to do nothing because you can't decide on the best, safest course of action. Unfortunately, doing nothing is exactly what led to the demise of corporations such as Blockbuster, Kodak, Woolworths, Pan Am, Lehman Brothers, Enron…

Imagine that you are a business. Your strategy is your career plan. You have no idea how it will work out. You might plan what your next move is going to be, what your next position might be but you don't know if you'll be successful, you don't know if that position will exist in a year's time. A year from now there will be positions that don't exist today. Should you wait? What if you move, and then an even better position turns up? How will it look if you move too often? How will it look if you don't move often enough?

All of these questions are not the questions of a rational mind. These questions are motivated by fear.

In our business analogy, shareholders are your supporters. These are people both inside and outside the business who have an interest in your success. What kind of people can you think of who are your supporters?

You might think of colleagues, leaders, family and friends.

Why do the leaders count? They know the future of the business is not them. They know that by the time you're in their leadership position they won't be here any more. They know that without you, the business has no future. You can't keep going back to the markets and hiring fresh people every year. One of the things that makes you valuable is the life-time of knowledge that's in your head and that means that you are unique. Other people can learn about technologies, other people can learn the business processes. None of that is difficult but the knowledge that is in your head took you a lifetime to acquire. Every day that knowledge makes your life easier but there will come a time when you have to somehow pass that knowledge on to the next generation of people.

Shareholders invest in your future and investment drives growth. If business shareholders invest money what do your supporters invest?

- Time

- Money

- Knowledge

Your shareholders are taking a gamble on you, hoping that you will help them beat the system. They invest in you because they expect a return on that investment. Your family might support your long working hours in the hope of a better quality of life in the future, for example.

Growth drives results. Results drive trust. You have people in your working life today who are your supporters, they care about your future success, they invest time and money and knowledge in your future success and the results you get today build trust, and that trust increases investment.

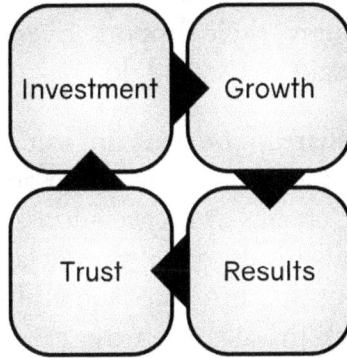

Simple. So are you doing that right now? Are you building trust in your future plans and communicating effectively with your shareholders? Or do you take the support that you receive for granted and assume that you can do whatever you please?

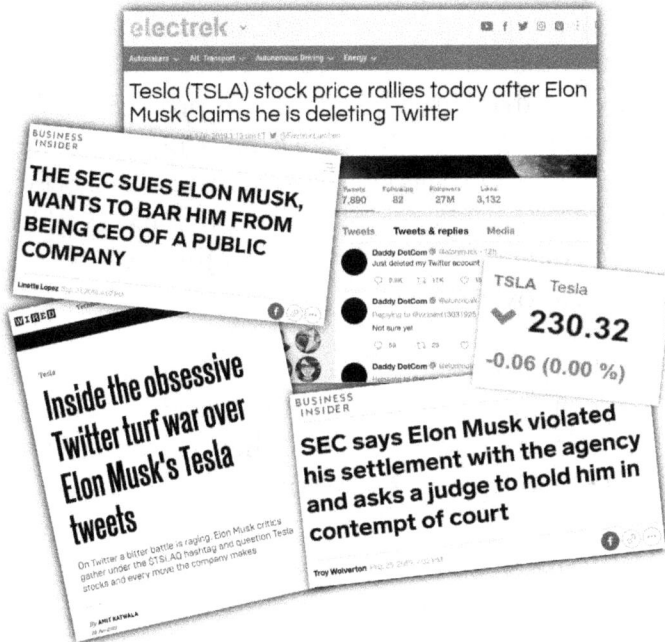

As soon as you raise investment based on a promise of future results, you are now accountable to your shareholders. You are no longer an individual, you are the representative and the core product of a community, a co-operative. You are now committed to your strategy because to change your mind or give up means that your investors don't see a return, and that could mean that they withdraw their support. Everyone is counting on you to do what you said you would do.

Just like company shares, you vary in value and your value is subjective. You get results today based on actions that you took in the past, and that creates an expectation about the future and that builds trust. Your results are always delayed because it takes time for your actions to turn into something measurable. For example, if you work in sales then the calls you made and the emails you sent six months ago might turn into the orders and the cash in the bank today.

What we know is that value takes a long time to build. You *could* go for an interview and say "I'm amazing, I can do all these great things, I'm a fantastic leader, I'm a great sales guy, I'm wonderful" and they *could* say "Okay, sounds good, we'll take a gamble", but you have to very quickly deliver on those promises. Real value, value that survives short term problems, takes a long time to build and past performance does not guarantee future results. Investment managers have to tell you that by law because our instinct is to say, "Wow, the share price has doubled in the last year, I'm going to make a fortune on this" Maybe not. Value can be destroyed overnight.

What's the biggest threat to your value? Artificial intelligence. Stopping evolving. Having limited experience. Creating a stock market crash in your own career. When you look at company share prices climbing very sharply and then crashing it's always because of loss of confidence caused by speculation and unfulfilled promises. You only have to read the financial news to see regular examples of this.

Investors' reaction to Volkswagen emissions saga

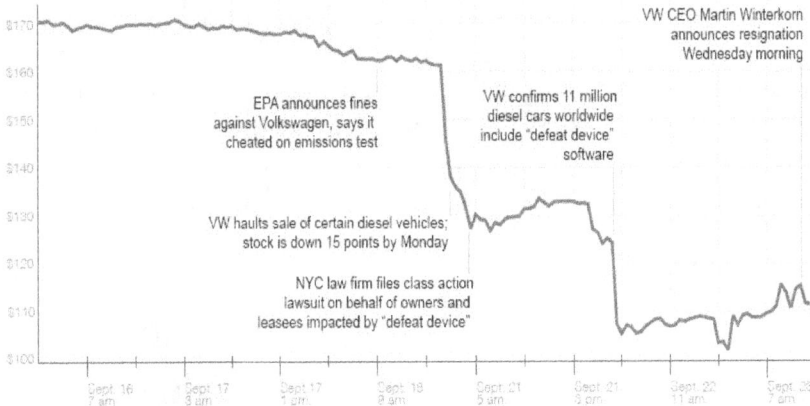

VW CEO Martin Winterkorn announces resignation Wednesday morning

EPA announces fines against Volkswagen, says it cheated on emissions test

VW confirms 11 million diesel cars worldwide include "defeat device" software

VW haults sale of certain diesel vehicles; stock is down 15 points by Monday

NYC law firm files class action lawsuit on behalf of owners and leasees impacted by "defeat device"

Source: Bloomberg

Stacy Jones, Fortune

On September 18th 2015, Volkswagen acknowledged the Environmental Protection Agency's emissions report. Shortly afterwards, the VW share price dropped sharply, and the fall seems to have been stopped temporarily by VW's action to halt sales of affected cars. However, when VW admitted using software to fool the emissions test, the share price dropped again. The price recovered slightly when the Chief executive resigned. Five days to end his career.

In March 2015, VW's share price hit 250€. Just a few months later in November, it crash-landed at 97€.

Why did that happen? Do you think any of these investors cared about the environment or the diesel emissions? This is what they care about: "VW halts sale of certain diesel models". Publicly, they'll say they care about the environment, but given the choice between saving a turtle and having some more cash in the bank? An individual human being will put cash in the bank. That is why our oceans are full of plastic. Every person who threw away one plastic bottle thought, "It's only one, what harm can it do?"

The oceans are polluted because that's human nature. That's why we have charities and government organisations to get people to talk to each other to work against human nature to solve the environmental problems that we have created for ourselves.

Think back to the experiment where three people predicted share prices. Critics said that comparing performance over such a short period of time is an unrealistic test, so let's look at VW's share price over a longer period of time, from 1998 to 2019:

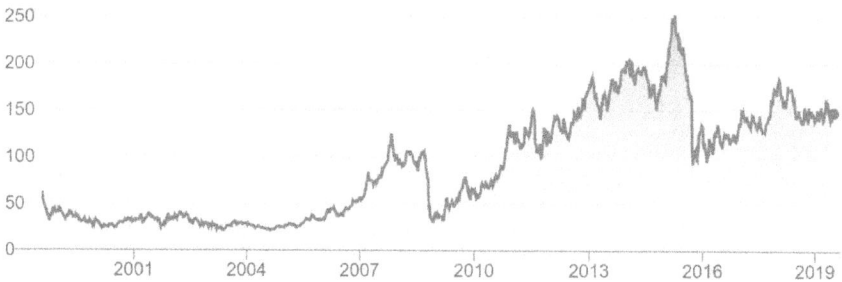

Source: Google

In terms of company value, that one little lie set the whole business back ten years. The drop in value in around 2008 is due to the Global Financial Crisis which affected everyone and reduced the value of the entire stock market. Some observers have blamed that catastrophe on the banks, who were lending money that they knew they would never get back, because the individual sales people were incentivised on loans sold, not loans repaid. The banks sold the debt to other banks but in the end, somebody had to pay. Lehman Brothers, in business since 1850, disappeared overnight.

VW's software worked by detecting the presence of an emissions test and adjusting the engine's fuel mixture. On the test bed, the car was cleaner, and on the road, it was more powerful. Everyone was happy. As soon as you introduce a rule, people will figure out how they can break it, how they can work round it to their own advantage. The engineers figured out a way to

Building Your Career Capital

deliver what the shareholders wanted – to sell more cars. No-one wanted to know how they did it.

As soon as you start measuring people, they will find ways to bend the rules because when you measure something, you create an expectation that more is better. As soon as you give someone a sales target you're setting an expectation that more is better, but that might not be the case. Your children won't grow any faster no matter how often you measure them.

Take a moment to think about how you're measured in your job. Think about your objectives, your goals, your targets, your KPIs. And now think about how 'hard' they are. What happens if you fall short of a target? Does anyone really care? And now think about the tricks you've learned to get round your targets.

One global business which we've worked closely with rewards managers for what they say they're going to do, not for what they actually did. This aligns with the organisation's obsession with quarterly stock market reports. By the time any of the new ideas and initiatives are supposed to deliver results, everyone has forgotten about them. Managers are rewarded for saying that they're going to win a project but no-one checks to see whether, a year or two later, that actually happened.

To increase your value, you show results, which you do in many different ways such as sales results and personal development reviews. You talk about your achievements, you talk about projects that you've delivered, you talk about your results. Your results are based on you selling something, or delivering a project, or creating something new, for example.

Your results are based on you doing the things you're paid to do, again, and again, and again. Before you know it, a year has gone by and you are still selling the same things and delivering the same things the same cycle has repeated, nothing has changed. You've proven time after time that you can really deliver and by doing that, you build a reputation, but for doing what? Achieving results, achieving goals, delivering the same thing over and over again. You build a reputation for being reliable, predictable, a solid performer. Not a rising star. It turns out that, in terms of your career progress, doing your job is completely counter-productive.

As soon as you want to change to a different position, move into a different business unit, you'll hear the inevitable question, "Do you have the experience? Have you done this job before? What experience do you have?" "None, that's why I want the job." That's scary for the investor. A risk, perhaps too big a risk.

Remember, the island is shrinking. If you're not moving forwards, your competitors are.

The challenge for you is that you achieve results because of what you do today. But you also have to think about networking and developing yourself and developing your teams and getting recognition, not for what you have done in the past, but for what you want to do in the future, and recognising in your teams what they're doing and building your succession plan.

The fundamental problem which faces you is building trust in what you say you're going to do in the future. If you have no platform of results to stand on, why should anyone trust you?

How did a computer manufacturer build trust in making mobile phones? How did an online bookshop redefine itself as a media producer?

In order to get from today to tomorrow we need a strategy and strategy needs investment. Building your career capital first means securing the investment to support your strategy.

Today / Tomorrow

Investment

If you're planning to move house, you need to sell one house at exactly the moment you buy another. If you want to buy before you've sold, you need something called a 'bridging loan', and they are expensive. Your lender expects a fast, secure return.

We start with investment, investment enables growth, growth delivers results, results deliver trust.

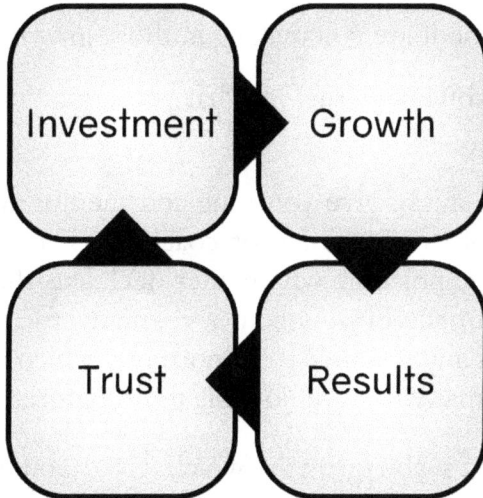

Investment → Growth

Trust ← Results

What you have to balance as you develop in your career is to deliver the results you're measured on today whilst also demonstrating that you are laying the foundations for the results you'll deliver tomorrow.

One of your biggest challenges is that you're not measured on what you'll deliver tomorrow, and you therefore don't receive visibility or recognition for that. It's not on anyone's dashboard, so if you don't measure it, if you don't publicise it, that value is lost. You have to be your own marketing expert.

Building Your Investment Plan Here are some questions for you to consider when building your career investment plan.

- What results are you measured on?

- Where are your growth areas in terms of your career development?

- What are the areas that you want to move into, where you don't have a proven history?

- What kind of investment would a supporter make to help you get across that gap in terms of growth areas?

- Where are your growth areas?

- What investment are you making in those growth areas?

- How is that building trust in what you are going to do in the future?

Your investors might give you time and mentoring. They might give you assignments, training or coaching. They might actually hire you into a position where they feel like they're taking a gamble. Investment in you comes in many forms, but it's all recognisable as any resource or opportunity which enables you to do something that you were not able to do before.

Investment gives you growth, which gives you results, which builds trust, which attracts investment. Trust isn't built on promises, it's built on results. The problem is when people see a pattern they will expect that pattern to continue in a straight line. When you deliver results, people will expect you to carry on delivering those results, but you don't want to carry on delivering those results, you want to do something different. You want a new opportunity and a new challenge, to develop your learning, to seek out new life and new civilisations, and so on.

Results have to be communicated. However, your regular reports and metrics are reflections of what you did weeks or months ago. No-one asks you to report on what you'll do in the future, so no-one knows your potential, and you don't get the recognition that builds trust and investment. Therefore, alongside your regular metrics and reports, you have to also create your own way of communicating your career strategy, just like a company communicates its intentions to the stock markets.

The people who have invested in your career strategy expect communication from you. They need to know that their investment has been a wise decision. They want to know what you're doing with the resources they've given you. And since your career progress is only possible thanks to their generous support, they deserve to know. If we strip this right down to the basics, what we're really talking about is immortality. One day, our frail, flawed human bodies will fail us. We will die. At the same time, we don't want to die. We want to live forever. We achieve immortality through legends and monuments and legacies. Not everyone will have a road or school prize or university building named after them, but we can all live on through the impact we make on future generations. You have read stories about ancient civilisations, kings and queens, historical figures. You have told stories about people who helped you when you were starting out on your career path. You have told stories about bad and good bosses, about mentors, and about important lessons you have learned. Just take a moment to consider what people in a similar position will be saying about you in thirty years time. Or sixty. Or a hundred. Or a thousand.

The people who invested in you live on through your stories.

This is the return on their investment in you.

Predicting Potential

Predicting potential is difficult for a very simple reason.

No matter how much effort you put into reviews, assessment centres and projects, the candidate knows they are being assessed, and their behaviour is oriented towards winning the approval of the assessor.

However, all of these assessments form a tiny part of the candidate's working life. They say all the right things and make themselves known to the right people, but their day job is where their time and attention are focused.

When a manager interviews an internal candidate, the manager is balancing the candidate's 'potential' against their performance in their current role.

When the interview assessment fits with data from the current role, the manager will perceive that the candidate represents a low risk in the role.

However, if the two are in conflict then the current data will outweigh whatever the candidate says in the interview.

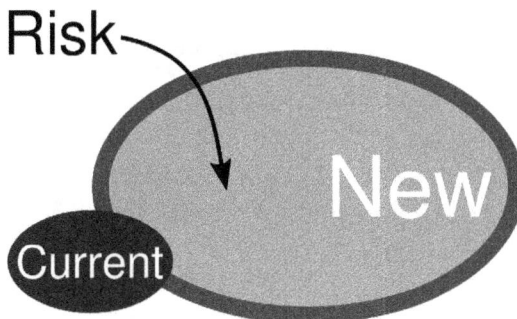

No matter how good the internal candidate sounds in the interview, the manager's primary experience is of them performing a job which is below the level of the role they are being considered for. The manager will find no evidence that they can 'step up' because that's the role they have been paid to do. Why would they have stepped up?

When a manager interviews an external candidate, they only have limited information upon which to base their judgement.

Even though the manager knows that people only write what they want others to read in their résumés, and they will only give good references and testimonials, the manager will still extrapolate what they hear from the candidate in the interview to form a picture of them in their current role, and their suitability for the role they're being interviewed for. Everything that the external candidate says "sounds good" because there is no context within which to evaluate the truth of their stories.

After the candidate has been selected and hired, they will usually perform well because that's just what people tend to do. In order for someone to be considered for a role, they can already perform that role, at least on paper. They will perform that role well, not because that is their capability, but because that is the position you place them in. They connect with the organisational inputs and outputs of their workflows. People send them emails, they send people emails. They are carried along in the fast-flowing current of organisational life. As long as they turn up to the office, they can't fail.

A sales manager in a pharmaceutical company told us about a new product launch where a recruitment agency was used to quickly hire a large number of temporary sales people to support the initial product launch. The agency conducted telephone interviews and hired based on the company's selection criteria. The manager met one of the candidates during a randomly selected sales meeting and discovered that the sales person could not speak a word of English. Someone else had written his application and taken the telephone interview.

Other than such obvious disconnects in the hiring process, you will find that human beings are capable of far more than they are given credit for, because expectations based on current behaviour cannot reliably be extrapolated to future challenges.

Self assessment

Consider this for a moment; are you capable of more than you are currently doing in your job? Are you ready for a bigger challenge, more responsibility? Are you more creative and capable than you are given credit for?

Rate yourself against this scale, where 1 is no challenge at all, no scope for creativity and no responsibility, 5 is a good balance and 9 is an overwhelming level of challenge.

For example, if your current role is a little boring, you might rate it a 3, and if your ideal role would present a high level of daily challenges, you might rate that a 9.

	1	2	3	4	5	6	7	8	9
Your current role									
Your capability									
Your ideal role									

If you've rated your capability as higher than your current role, the next obvious question is, what makes you special? Why wouldn't everyone else be as under-rated as you are?

When you predict a person's potential, you have to imagine them performing in a future role, based on the limited information that you have about them now.

A hiring manager will generally have more information about an internal candidate than about an external candidate, and that puts the external candidate at an advantage.

Of course, you can ask the external candidate for a reference from their current employer, but you'll only do that once you've decided to hire them, and even then, if they were a poor performer their old employer will jump at the chance to get rid of them. You might ask for other references earlier on in the selection process, but the candidate will only provide the names of people who will give them the best reference.

You could use various psychometric tools to get a clearer picture of the candidate, but they all have their limitations, and of course they can only make generalised predictions about a candidate, based on their past experience.

The simple fact is that unless you have observed someone in a senior role over an extended period of time, you have no idea how they will really perform, and that uncertainty represents a risk. The higher the hiring manager perceives that risk to be, the less likely they are to hire that candidate.

Your focus has to be on balancing those risks. Too many candidates focus on proving that they are the best, and on making wild promises about their future performance which are useless and completely unverifiable. What every hiring manager is trying to do is make a 'safe' prediction about the future, and therefore they generally do not hire the 'best' candidate, they hire who they perceive to be the safest.

You do exactly the same thing when you're choosing a restaurant for a special occasion. Rather than try a new restaurant, you are more likely to go somewhere familiar, or at least to test out a new restaurant first. You would try to balance the risks by soliciting reviews from people you trust, and you would spend hours reading online reviews, focusing on the low-scoring reviews to see if they represent isolated problems or if they reveal some kind of systemic failing that you can build into your prediction.

The risks that you are aiming to balance are:

Will the special occasion be special enough?	v	Will the restaurant let me down?

In other words, you could make the occasion very special indeed by arranging a private table at the top of the Eiffel Tower after all the tourists have gone, however there are so many variables that this represents a risk. On the other hand, you could settle for the absolute certainty of McDonald's, but it probably wouldn't feel very special. You feel good that you have made the 'right' decision when these risks are balanced.

The hiring manager has the same challenge. He or she can't afford to make a mistake, because he or she does not want to repeat the process, and employment law usually makes this difficult anyway. Recruiters try to minimise risk with psychometric assessments (which they don't understand how to use) and assessment centres (which they don't understand how to run) and, in the end, they fall back on their gut instinct anyway.

What the hiring manager doesn't realise is that every hiring decision they make is wrong. Hiring the right candidate has little to do with the selection process; the induction and development phase is far more important to align the new hire with the culture of the organisation. Cultural alignment is the most important factor in the performance of an individual. In short, if you can't play in a team, it doesn't really matter how good you are on your own.

The hiring manager will act as if you are the only person they will ever hire, and they will put themselves under more pressure to make the right decision. The bad news for you is that this tips the risk balance greatly in favour of a candidate who represents a 'safe pair of hands', and so it would be wise for you to present yourself in this way.

In an ideal world, the recruiter would hire someone who has done the exact same job before, in a similar company, in a similar market, and who has consistently over-achieved against their targets. There is only one place where this type of candidate exists, and that is in the imagination of the recruitment agency when they rewrite your CV/resumé and pitch you to their client.

When a manager compares internal and external candidates, the balance of risks between them is different. The internal candidate is proven in the wrong role, and the external candidate is unproven in the right role. Both candidates are telling stories about what they *could* and *would* and *might* do, and the manager is trying to do what we all do in any decision; balance the risks in order to reduce the size of the gap between present and future.

In short, no candidate is a completely safe bet. However, the risks involved are not objective measures, they are perceptions and you can easily uncover the risks perceived by the hiring manager during the interview, and align your skills accordingly in order to tip the balance back in your favour.

Demonstrating Your Strengths

As a candidate for a more senior position, you have the problem of trying to prove your potential to do more than your colleagues and managers know you for.

The paradox is that your potential is in the perception of others, therefore it's a combination of what you do and what others think about what you do, and you can't control what others think because their perception is based on their own life experiences.

By definition, you cannot demonstrate your potential, you can only demonstrate your capability. Potential is the area of your capability which you have not yet shown, and as soon as you show it, it's not potential any more, it's what you're actually doing. Your potential therefore exists only as a promise in the imaginations of others, and as soon as you attempt to deliver on that promise, you break it because whatever you do is 'not quite what they had in mind'.

Have you ever fantasised, only to be disappointed when your fantasy finally became reality? Have you imagined what a food or place or experience would be like, only to find that the reality fell far short of your expectations? Many career and self-help experts promise to 'unlock your potential', but your potential is actually more valuable to you when it is safely locked away.

Most people will attempt to show 'potential' by seeking out new projects and challenges. This depends on the opportunities being available to do that, and of course how much free time you have from your 'day job'. If you simply take on more work, you'll be recognised for being willing to take on more work, and guess what your reward will be? More work. The world is not short of busy people. What we need more of is smart people.

If you regularly seek out new opportunities, you will earn yourself a reputation as someone who eagerly takes on new work whilst still on your current salary. A dog who eagerly runs to catch a stick shows no potential to herd sheep.

That's probably not the reputation that you're aiming for.

You can simply focus on the qualities that you demonstrate in your every day work and then manage the perception of what you're doing, in the same way that marketing professionals manage our perception of their fine products and services. In other words, do your job, but make it look better than it really is.

Let's consider another example – customer service. Have you ever been given more than you asked for, perhaps to make up for some perceived problem from the service provider? Imagine that you order a book and it takes longer to arrive than the retailer initially indicated. To apologise for the delay, they send you another book as a gift. However, they didn't know that you were away from home, and you have no idea when the book arrived. The free gift is very welcome, yet unnecessary.

In 2012, The University of Maryland conducted some research entitled, "Linkages between customer service, customer satisfaction and performance in the airline industry"

This research found that the connection between service and profit is 'non-linear', in other words, it's not a simple, direct connection, where more customer service = more profit.

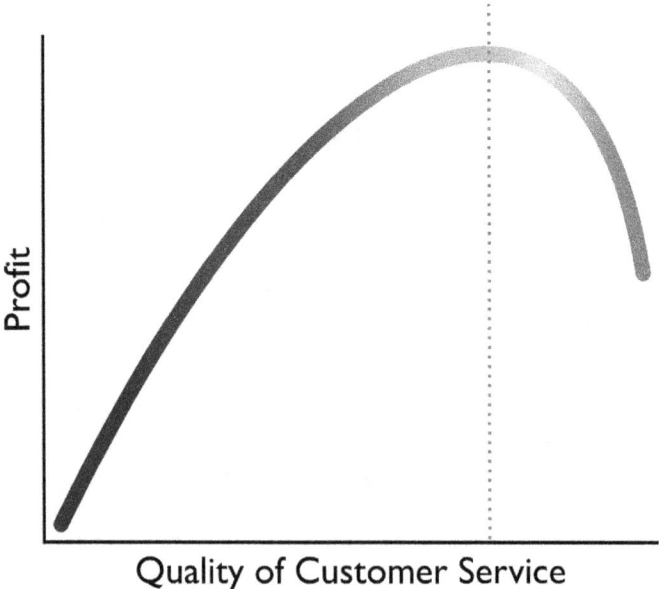

Quality of Customer Service

Demonstrating Your Strengths

It seems that better service leads to increased profits up to a certain point, and then it doesn't matter how much better your service is, your profits decline because the additional service activities do not influence the customer's perception, and those extra activities cost money.

The parallel between this research and the candidate's desire to demonstrate their potential is that they can very easily take on more work, and spend more time on new tasks which go unnoticed. This is counter-productive because the candidate now has less time to spend on the activities which actually are important.

In the service example, service providers will provide additional benefits or concessions which they believe will lead to customer satisfaction and therefore increased customer retention. However, the service provider does what they think the customer wants, not what actually makes a difference to the customer. A service provider might give you a discount that you haven't asked for, or might offer you some free accessories which you don't need. A car dealer might offer you coffee and biscuits while you wait in their executive lounge, when all you want is to get out of there as quickly as possible.

Similarly, in trying to demonstrate potential, many candidates do work which is unnecessary, to an unnecessarily high standard. Hiring managers may not notice at all, or they may come to expect this behaviour as normal. Once you get a discount from your favourite restaurant, you expect it every time. You were going to visit the restaurant anyway, so the only thing that the owner has achieved is to give away profit. The candidate simply gives away their time and effort, and gains no advantage.

A retail client in the UK responded to increasing competition by having special sales days, with 15% off all of their prices. Average store managers put the sales leaflets in with customer order deliveries, thereby giving 15% discount to existing customers who were already buying from the retailer. Their measure of success was how many leaflets they sent out.

A handful of smart managers delivered leaflets to local companies that were not currently buying from the retailer. One manager saw an increase in profits of 485% by doing this.

On the other hand, doing a good job and waiting to get noticed is not enough, because there are candidates who are making more noise, who are better positioned and who are getting noticed first. They may not be the best candidate for the position, but they are in the right place at the right time.

If every manager in every retailer adopted the same approach, potential customers would be overwhelmed with leaflets and there would be no net gain for any one retailer. In order to make a difference, you have to do something different.

A LinkedIn post from a prominent UK CEO illustrates the point: "We had a good laugh that some agencies still send balloons in boxes and think it's original."

In the centre of the Moroccan city of Tangiers, tradesmen wait every morning by the side of the road, hoping to be hired for a day's work. Each sits beside a board displaying their talents. The board doesn't list their talents, it showcases them. The electricians display neatly arranged wiring, the plumbers display a variety of pipes and the builders display a panel of bricks or tiles.

In first world economies, tradesmen join trade associations, or the government mandates certifications which prove capability. The customer cannot tell the difference between a good or a bad electrician, so they trust the certifying body to make that distinction. In Tangiers, the customer can see the tradesman's work on the board, although of course someone else could have made that for them. The tradesmen are being hired for a day at a time, so if the customer picks the wrong person, all they've lost is a day's work. If the board members of a global bank pick the wrong CEO, the mistake might take longer to correct.

When making decisions, we all face the same problem, which is to gather information that will help us make the decision whilst minimising the risk of making the wrong decision. We try to restrict unnecessary information, for fear of confusing the issue.

The challenge for you as a candidate is to do your job well and to demonstrate your best capabilities to hiring managers without taking on unnecessary work that makes no difference to your career development yet raises expectations of the volume of work that you will do in the future.

Prioritising

If you don't know what to focus on to demonstrate your best capabilities, this exercise will help you.

- If you had only 1 week per month in which to do your job, what would you focus on?

- If you had only 1 day per month in which to do your job, what would you focus on?

- If you had only 1 hour per month in which to do your job, what would you focus on?

- If you had only 1 minute per month in which to do your job, what would you focus on?

This is your order of priorities.

There are many psychometric profiling tools which promise to show you your strengths. The idea is that by focusing on your strengths, you will be more motivated and productive because you are doing what you're naturally good at. Similarly, you should minimise the time spent in areas of weakness.

These types of test are very attractive, for the same reason that people love to know what their horoscope sign says about them. However, they are flawed in one very important respect, which is the concept that a person has strengths and weaknesses. From a humanistic perspective, a person has life experiences, interests, likes, dislikes and preferences.

None of these is a strength or a weakness in itself, and these judgements say more about the context and the observer than the person being observed. For example, an entrepreneur might fail in a business venture and immediately start another. An observer looking for strengths might say that the entrepreneur has the strength of persistence, yet from the entrepreneur's point of view, he or she might feel that they have no choice but to start again. They are not persistent, they are doing the only thing that they know how to do in order to pay the bills.

If you look for strengths, you'll surely find them, and the same goes for weaknesses. Again, from a humanistic perspective, a weakness is nothing more than a strength taken out of context. What, therefore, makes a person successful is not their strengths, it is their situational awareness.

There's an old joke about an engineer who charges a customer $100 for fixing a heating system by hitting it with a hammer. The customer feels that this is a high price for such a small job and demands an itemised bill.

REPAIR BILL

For tapping with hammer:

$1

For knowing where to tap:

$99

Yes, it's important that you demonstrate your strengths but it's equally important that you do what makes you happy. There are countless things that you are good at, but do you want to have to do them every day?

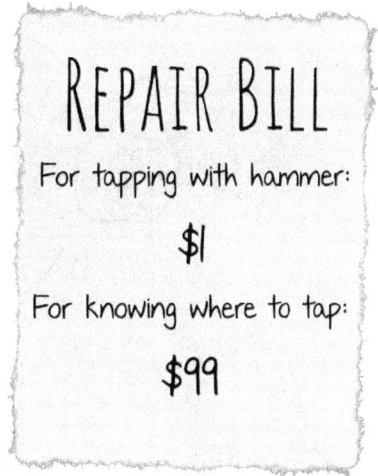

Here's another way of looking at the issue of strengths – a strength is anything that you use often. If you use a muscle it gets stronger. Your mind and body are built upon a system which self-reinforces parts which are used more. City planners know about this concept too. They create foot paths and car parks and areas of grass and bushes, and it all looks beautiful on their plans. However, once people start interacting with the space, those plans get rewritten. People walk where they want to walk, not where the planners want them to walk. The more a path gets used, the more worn it becomes, the more visible it becomes, and the more people use it.

The simplest way to look at this is as follows. Do what you enjoy, because if you enjoy it you'll want to do it more often, and if you do it more often you'll get better at it, and when you get better at it, people will reward you more for doing it. Recognition and feeling valued fuels your enjoyment.

Demonstrating your strengths is therefore not quite as simple as seeking out opportunities to do what you're good at, because what you're good at today is what you were rewarded for yesterday. Building your career capital requires you to focus on what you want to be rewarded for tomorrow, and that means that you will need a different set of strengths. For example, as a first line manager, you need to be able to motivate a small team, but as a senior manager, you aren't managing the people directly doing 'the work', you are managing other managers. You need new skills, including strategic thinking and long-term planning to enable you to execute a complex strategy through a large team. The idea of doing this might seem daunting at first, and you might think that the more practice you get, the more confident you become, and that is certainly true. The problem is that the career decision maker isn't paying you to practice, they are paying you to deliver. They want you to start with ready-made skills so that their hiring decision is as low a risk as possible.

Adaptability is therefore one of the most important strengths to develop, and if we consider what that actually means, it doesn't mean that you're good at whatever you turn your hand to, it means that you are willing to throw yourself into an unfamiliar situation, draw upon your own experience, accept help from others, solicit feedback, learn fast and make it work.

Notice that we don't say that 'you're not afraid to try something new', because adaptable people *are* afraid. They simply know that their fear of the unknown, or failure, or criticism, or rejection, is their fear, based on their own life experiences. Just because they doubt themselves doesn't mean that other people doubt them. They have learned not to be stopped by their fear.

To demonstrate that you can develop new strengths, you have to be willing to put yourself into new situations that you have never encountered before. When a manager asks for a volunteer to take on a new project, or present to an important customer, or lead an innovation team, you cannot afford to be the person hiding at the back of the room. Your hand has to be the first in the air.

Be Seen

You may have been told to improve your career prospects by increasing your visibility. That's not enough. Anyone can create visibility. The well-known phrase 'no publicity is bad publicity' is hard to attribute to any one author, though it's similar in spirit to Oscar Wilde's observation that, "The only thing worse than being talked about is not being talked about."

You also need to think about what you want to be visible for.

On top of that, what you think you're showing might not be what other people are seeing. You might think of asking people for feedback on that, however it is often unlikely that other people will be honest with you. Why wouldn't people want to help you with honest feedback?

- They don't want to hurt your feelings

- They are uncomfortable voicing a personal opinion

- They don't want to help you

- They see you as a competitor

These tendencies will make people give you feedback which is pleasant, neutral and ultimately unhelpful. What you really need to do is gain feedback from other people's behaviour towards you. How they treat you reveals what they think of you.

Another problem with visibility is that an organisational culture which rewards it can create a 'glass ceiling' which we'll discuss later on. In short, such a visibility driven culture can create a situation where people are rewarded for being seen, not for doing a good job or getting results. This is common in an organisational culture that only measures medium term results such as annual sales figures, because managers have no way to measure the short term behaviours that lead to those annual results, so instead they focus on what appear to be the signs of someone 'doing the right things', such as going to lots of important meetings and commenting on their manager's nice new car. We've often heard managers criticise their teams for not speaking up enough in meetings, regardless of whether they had anything valuable to add or not.

Any manager can create any measures for their teams that they want, at any time, but few managers do this consciously. It's more common that the manager informally rewards the behaviours that they unconsciously approve of, such as agreeing with the manager during meetings and working late.

Many people feel uncomfortable with the concept of visibility because it sounds a lot like organisational politics; saying and doing the right things to get ahead, instead of just doing a good job. Unfortunately, we live in a competitive world, and when everyone else is doing a good job too, there is little to differentiate one job candidate from another. You have to do something to stand out from the crowd. The good news is that if everyone else in the crowd is trying to stand out then you don't need to compete on the same level. The key to understanding the concept of visibility is to think in very simple terms about what the word means – to be visible means that something is seen by someone. Therefore, for you to work on your visibility, you have to think about what you want to be seen for, and who you want to be seen by.

While your competitors are working on their politics, you can carefully target the people you want to be seen by, your career stakeholders. You could think of them as investors, because they will invest their time and resources in your future. When investors put money into a company to fund its growth, they expect more money back at some future time. Your career stakeholders are working in reverse; they are investing in you to repay the investment that someone else made in them. Your stakeholders are not necessarily decision makers or senior managers, they could be anyone who has a vested interest in your success and the connections or resources to help you.

To begin building your investment strategy, you can start by drawing a stakeholder map. It's a very simple diagram that compares two factors: how much influence a person has on your career, and how often you have contact with them.

You'll see your family and friends often, and they are important in supporting you, however their direct influence on the outcome of your next job application is likely to be low. The decision maker for your next role has a high influence, but you probably don't have regular contact with them. It may be that you have no communication with them at all – yet.

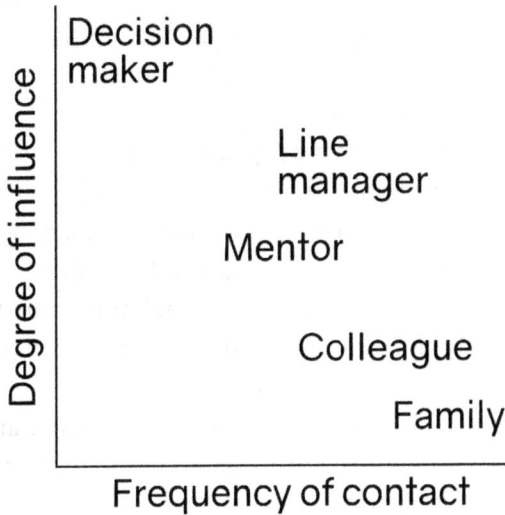

Once you've drawn your stakeholder map, your next task is to work out a contact strategy. You might think that this means you only talk to people who have high influence, but that's not the case. As in any sales strategy, you have to use the decision maker at the right time, not just spend all your time with them. If they're a decision maker, all of your competitors want their time and attention too. If you don't plan carefully, you'll be lost in that background noise. A decision maker is only influential when they are making a decision, and at all other times, they could actually present a hindrance, barrier or even a threat. Sales people are often so focused on getting in front of decision makers that they forget this simple fact – that most of the time, decision makers are not making decisions. Imagine a restaurant owner trying to convince you to try a fabulous new dish created by their chef. As mouth-watering and tantalising as it may be, when you're at home watching TV, the restaurant owner's words of encouragement becomes irrelevant noise. When you're driving to work, their words go in one ear and out of the other. When you're sitting in the restaurant with the menu in your hands, that's the only time that their recommendation has any influence over your decision. Therefore, identifying the decision makers for your career is important, but what's more important is recognising when they are in a position to value your input.

The higher the frequency of contact with someone, the greater your opportunity to build the perception you want through honest, consistent behaviour. The more time you spend with someone, the harder it is to keep up an act. If you're pretending to be someone you're not in order to get a job, there will be a discontinuity between what the decision maker sees and what your line manager, for example, sees. For external roles, there will be a discontinuity between your behaviour in the interview and your social media presence, and this has been a big problem for many candidates, so much so that many now hide their identity online with alternative versions of their names, perhaps using their middle names or nicknames. Of course, smart recruiters have many more ways of finding out what you're really like, and the higher you progress in your career, the more information is available about you. Instead of trying to hide this information, make sure it aligns with who you really are. Any misalignment will be discovered, and will not serve you well.

Another important point about frequency of contact is that if you have only 10 seconds in front of the decision maker in that clichéd moment in the elevator, all of the pressure for your entire career progress rests on that moment. It's no wonder that you've been told to practice your elevator pitch in the hope that one day, you'll be in that position.

Incidentally, don't bother with an elevator pitch. Cramming your life story and all the reasons to hire you or buy from you into ten seconds is like an advert on the radio. The decision maker isn't listening, and everyone else is doing it. Instead, if you do happen to cross paths with someone who you would like to spend more time with, simply tell them that. Say who you are and ask for 15 minutes of their time. That's it. Most of the time, they will agree because a critical part of their role is to identify and nurture future leaders. The fact that you haven't bombarded them with a contrived and irritating elevator pitch is a bonus. If they can't say yes because they need to know more about you, they will ask for the information you need. They might even refer you to someone else who is actually better suited towards supporting your objectives.

Returning to the issue of visibility, it might seem like the solution is simply to do your job well, and that is certainly important because ultimately it's why you were hired, it's what you're paid to do, and it's what your manager, colleagues and customers rely on you to do. However, if everyone is doing a good job, you still need to solve the problem of how to stand out from the crowd. You have to assume that everyone around you is at least as competent as you, simply because they were hired by the same people using the same selection processes. If you think that your colleagues are idiots, you might want to check in the mirror before going any further.

Back in the restaurant, if you're having trouble choosing from the menu, it's because it *all* looks good, and it all looks good because it was all created and described by the same person with the same intention in mind – to make you want it. There is nothing in the menu that will help you to choose. You have to rely on your own experience of what you enjoy. If you're really stuck, you'll ask the waiter to make a recommendation, and then you're relying on their opinion, and your trust in them. Once again, trust becomes a substitute for information.

Your stakeholder map will inform your choices, because your aim should be to focus on the people who sit in the centre of the map. You have enough contact that they feel confident in their perception of you, and they have enough influence that they will be asked to share their perceptions of you with decision makers.

Candidates who only focus on impressing the most senior manager are fundamentally trying to avoid the hard work of networking, and the hard work of doing their jobs. Senior managers are usually experienced enough to spot these kinds of candidates, mainly because they see so many of them, so you might wonder why they are still successful in getting ahead on the basis of organisational politics alone.

There are two simple reasons for this. The first is that the decision maker might not want someone who does a good job, their criteria might be to hire someone for some other reason. The second reason is that people who play political games are easily manipulated, and are perfect footsoldiers for empire builders who like to surround themselves with 'yes men'. If that's the character of the decision maker then in reality you're not well suited to working for them if your intention is to work hard and do a good job. If your intention is to get to the top as easily as possible then rest assured, you will pay the price later when the empire collapses. Political empires within organisations always collapse because, ultimately, shareholders want cash, not empty promises, which means that hard organisational targets have to be achieved at some point. Empire builders have a tendency to surround themselves with 'yes men', and because this has the effect of insulating the leader from bad news, they never find out about operational problems until those problems are out of control. The time spent fire-fighting, covering up and figuring out how to report operational data is time that could be spent on activities that actually achieve the targets that the 'yes men' are trying to fake.

In one UK based engineering company, losses of £16 million a year were estimated based only on project delay penalties and the cost of contract staff. The layer of senior managers were more focused on covering up their failures than on putting things right. In one failed 'employee engagement' scheme, all 250 staff were offered a £1000 productivity bonus if they hit their targets at the end of the year. The end of the year came, performance was still nowhere near targets and the bonus was paid anyway because 'people had come to expect it'. In other words, managers wanted it, and couldn't justify only paying themselves, so since it wasn't their quarter of a million, pay it anyway. There was also the small factor that the company, part of a global conglomerate, was misreporting its performance to the global board by fabricating project reports and using statistical tricks to make financial results look better than they actually were. Their Australian division was also managed by the UK company, and so the Australian results, which were consistently good, were hidden within the UK figures in order to raise the average.

Situations like this, and Enron, and Worldcom, Freddie Mac, GE, Carillion, AIG, BCCI and Tesco all raise the same questions – why didn't anyone know about the fraud? Why did no-one say anything? Why didn't the problem come to light sooner?

The answer is simply that the people who knew about what was going on were also benefiting from it – up until the point that it got serious, when they then benefited from covering it up. The individual pieces of the puzzle don't make any sense to the people 'lower down' and the big picture doesn't look good to the people 'higher up'. Most people will see an error on an expenses claim, a missed deadline, an unusual budget approval. Nothing to worry about. One-offs, mistakes, oversights. Once we get far enough up the organisation to put those puzzle pieces together, we're already complicit in the conspiracy. No-one found out about the problems because no-one was supposed to, until the problems got so big that they could no longer be hidden.

For you and your career strategy, you can see that there are many easy routes to the top, but they are fraught with danger. The safe path for your career is the same as the safe path for mountain climbers – it's the path that has the most places to land safely when you fall off. It's inevitable that you will fall off. Your employer will go out of business for, hopefully, no fault of your own. Your division might be divested and sold to a competitor. Your team might be made redundant. You might get six months notice of such changes at best, giving you time to hastily plan your next step, increase your networking activity and, if necessary, get on the phone to the recruitment agencies. If you're unlucky, these changes will seem to happen overnight. Of course, that's never the case, you simply weren't informed, which meant that you weren't connected. This is another good reason to network continually. Leaders who are invested in your career will give you advance notice of changes that are likely to affect you, because what affects you affects them.

Being seen is easy, but it's not enough. You have to think about what you want to be seen for, what you want to be recognised for. Focus on that, and getting yourself seen will be much less of a problem.

Seeing the Future

A hiring manager or decision maker is, as we have already said, trying to make a reliable prediction about the future. They are trying to match you to their internal expectation of what a 'high potential' looks like. We've conducted some research into this and found some consistent qualities that they look for, which we'll discuss later in the book. For now, it's important to develop a different skill – that of looking inside the mind of the decision maker.

The decision maker, like any buyer, does not want to tell the sales person what they really want, because they don't want their independent decision to be influenced. They want to see your cards without showing you theirs.

Your challenge is that the decision maker knows exactly what they're looking for, regardless of what their recruitment competency framework or psychometric profiling system tells them. In fact, they knew who they were looking for, long before they interviewed you. In fact, they knew who they were looking for, long before they even knew they had a position to recruit for. This is because of two important reasons, both of which are critical for your career success.

The first reason is that human beings based their decisions on their past experiences, and the template for every decision you will ever make was created long in the past. That template will almost never change. Thanks to the cognitive biases which we've already mentioned, the earliest and best template that you have for a trustworthy, honest, reliable, hard-working, good person is, of course, yourself.

The second reason is that human beings are convinced that they know what's going on in each other's minds, when in reality, what they're doing is projecting their own mind onto other people. Humans are not the only animals to do this, primates, dogs, elephants, dolphins and even some birds have the same ability. In short, people expect everyone to think the way that they do, and people expect everyone to like what they like.

The first reason drives predictable consistency in the decision making process of a recruiter. If you learn that process, you can influence it.

The second reason means that the decision maker will, essentially, aim to recruit themselves, or at least someone who reminds them of themselves.

In our research, which we describe in more detail later in this book, we found a remarkable consistency in the qualities that a person looks for in a perfect candidate, and the qualities that a person believes are the reasons for their own success.

In short, if you admire the quality of punctuality in yourself, you will describe it as a generally desirable quality, and you will look for it in others as a sign of 'high potential', when in reality, it may be irrelevant, and it may not be one of the specific criteria you're recruiting for. If someone wants to be admired by you, all they have to do is turn up on time.

This tendency crops up time and time again in decades of psychology research, from the Simulation Theory of Mind Reading to the Dunning-Kruger effect.

What you really want to know is how to use this information to your advantage in the recruitment process.

Let's start with the first reason outlined above; predictability. Simply, if you look at a recruiter's track record of decisions, you will be able to notice patterns, driven by their unconscious biases and prejudices. Corporate recruitment procedures are designed to remove such personal biases, however decision makers will usually find a way to 'tick the boxes' and still get the candidate they want. Such a bias doesn't guarantee a decision, but it's a strong indicator. It typically won't be as obvious as a bias for students of a particular business school, or ex-employees of a certain type of organisation, however these biases certainly do influence the decision. Malcolm Gladwell, in his book 'Blink', uses the term 'thin slicing' to refer to the mental shortcuts that

Seeing the Future

we use to make complex decisions. The idea is that we make big, complex decisions quickly, based on very small amounts of data which we have learned are representative of the 'right criteria'.

For example, a candidate who is punctual must have good time management skills and must be well organised, and will therefore be a reliable employee. The logic seems good, but this explanation of the importance of punctuality is not entirely true. When asked to justify why punctuality is important, the decision maker may well use this kind of logic, which seems very sensible, however the real reason for their bias towards a punctual candidate is that they believe that punctuality is a sign of deference or respect, and that tells you that the decision maker's underlying bias is based on their needs for status and power. A recruiter without that need would be more likely to excuse a candidate's lateness by agreeing that the traffic is terrible, and the office is hard to find, and it's OK because we're running a little late anyway.

What you can now see is that the recruiter's bias towards certain decision patterns is not as simple as it first seems, because we also need to know the underlying reasons or drivers for that bias. However once you know what to look for, the bias becomes obvious. It also creates a paradox, which leads on to the second reason.

The recruiter who has a need for power and status will be attracted to this quality in others, but will also compete with it. You're sure to have been in meetings or business events where you've observed two people competing with each other, perhaps by listing their most impressive credentials, or describing the powerful or famous people they've met.

The recruiter is fundamentally looking for someone who exhibits the same traits that got them to where they are. If they believe that the secret of their success is their willingness to learn, then they're looking for someone who is willing to learn. How can you prove to them that you are willing to learn? Perhaps a list of training courses that you've attended? Or something more subtle, such as a willingness to learn in the interview, evidenced by your delight in what the interviewer tells you, and your keen questioning to discover more?

The problem that you face is that the recruitment advert and job description were probably written by someone in HR, and those documents bear almost no relation to what the decision maker is *really* looking for. At each step of the recruitment process, you must look no further than the decision immediately in front of you, and that means focusing on the decision maker for each stage of the process. The HR advisor is not a gatekeeper, they are a decision maker for their stage of the overall process. Every person who you talk to is integral to your success.

This brings us back to reason one; understanding the consistent process. You can't only focus on the ultimate decision maker, you have to focus on each intermediate decision maker that stands between you and career aspirations.

Let's step inside the mind of the decision maker. They don't know you, they only know what you reveal to the outside world. They will take the snippets of information which you choose to reveal and piece those together, filling in the gaps from their own experiences. What they end up with is a complete picture which either makes them feel that you're a 'good fit' for the role, or leaves them with enough doubt to overlook your application.

How, exactly, do they do that?

It's incredibly simple, and it's something that you do yourself. Imagine that you want to buy a new piece of furniture, or a gift for a loved one. How do you make your decision? You might say that, "You just know" which is the right choice. Well, if we could only rely on the recruiter 'just knowing' then that wouldn't be very helpful. There has to be more to it.

Think about something that you have bought recently, where you couldn't try out the item before buying it. For example, an item of furniture, an accessory for your car, a gift for someone else, an item of clothing that you couldn't try on in the shop. If you were ultimately happy with your purchase then what you probably did is to picture, in your mid, that purchase in its intended location. You imagined the furniture in your home. You imagined your loved one opening the gift. You created a prediction, an imaginary representation of the future. As you looked at the item of furniture in your imaginary home, you checked if it would fit, if the colour scheme looked good, if it would offer you the right storage space, and so on. You took a list of criteria, and you applied those criteria to the potential purchase, all inside your imagination. This is what your brain is built to do, and this is exactly what the recruiting decision maker will do.

The decision maker will create an imaginary future scenario, place you in it and create a mental movie which allows them to observe your behaviour, and they will then check that behaviour against their list of criteria.

The problem for you is this: They don't tell you that they're doing that, because they're not consciously aware of it, and you therefore don't have an opportunity to correct any misunderstandings that they may have. If they have not observed a certain trait or quality in you, they can't project it into their imaginary future, and they will feel that you don't meet their requirements for the role. They will even say, "I just can't see you in the role". They are speaking quite literally. They cannot visualise you performing to their expectations. You might feel that this is an unfair assessment, which is irrelevant. You did not show them what they needed to see.

Here's an actual example from a leadership talent program. One of the nominated 'high potentials' walked into the room where the program participants were gathering. He stood, looking around the room, apparently not sure who to talk to, and appeared hesitant to approach any of the groups who were already in conversation. The Regional VP was also in the room.

Afterwards, the Regional VP commented that the participant seemed 'out of his depth' and 'lost', and said that he 'couldn't see' that person as a candidate for a leadership position.

We later met with and interviewed the VP, who revealed that his most highly valued personal quality was that he very quickly 'gets under the skin' in a new situation, and when asked how he does that, he replied that he very quickly asks lots of detailed questions about what's happening. Projecting this externally, he's looking for that exact same behaviour in his 'high potentials'. The participant in question may have had other, excellent leadership qualities, which were all irrelevant. He couldn't be observed asking questions, and consequently he wasn't 'leadership material'.

On further analysis, the VP said that he imagines a future scenario where a particular region or business unit is struggling, and imagines the candidate going in to 'fix' that situation, which typically means to pull the commercial performance back on track. In other words, he visualises the candidate performing a 'troubleshooter' role, and looks to see if he can imagine the candidate performing the actions which the VP believes are most critical to success in the role.

Guess what the VP sees himself as, and what roles his career is built around? Commercial troubleshooter.

How does the VP know what qualities he values most in himself? Because they are the qualities that he has been rewarded for in his career.

People talk about 'self worth' but in reality, you cannot have self worth, because you cannot value yourself, you can only value another, or feel valued by another. So the things that you do in order to get approval or acceptance or reward are the things that you have been valued for throughout your life. If, as a child, you were called a "clever boy" or a "smart girl" then these are the qualities which you will most seek to exhibit, and which you will seek out reward and recognition for. This means that the most successful roles in your career are the ones where your most valued qualities are most in demand, and most rewarded.

When you go to an interview, you feel under pressure, which pushes you into your comfort zone, and you want to show yourself in what you think is your best light, so you will aim to exhibit these qualities most strongly, but they may not be the qualities that matter to the interviewer. In fact, it's very unlikely. You might think that this means you have to pretend to be someone you're not in order to get the job, but that's not true. You simply have to shift your focus, because you have many more valuable qualities than the ones you might naturally want to portray, and in reality it's highly unlikely that you will have day to day contact with the interviewer once you're hired. Therefore, you can shift your focus onto the qualities which they value, knowing that once you're in the role, you can focus back on the qualities which you value most. Or, you can take the opportunity to realise that you have many more valuable qualities than the ones you have restricted yourself to in the past. Or, you might even find that, in a different organisational culture, different qualities are rewarded and your priorities change.

Read through this section again carefully, because it tells you everything you need to know to influence the recruiter. Here are some key reminders for you:

- The decision maker will base their own value on what they have been recognised for in the past

- They will then project those valuable qualities onto their 'ideal candidate'

- They will imagine you in a future scenario that exploits those qualities and try to imagine those qualities in you

- If they can imagine those behaviours, they conclude that you're a good fit for the role

In short, they look at what you're doing now, and if it aligns with the qualities they value in themselves, they project those behaviours into the future and consider you to be a 'high potential'

You might think that it would take a long time to understand the decision maker's criteria, and that you would have to get to know them personally to discover their most valued experiences.

Fortunately, that's not the case, and in fact it is very easy to find out, once you realise the simple fact that everyone's favourite subject is themselves, and every successful person's favourite subject is the secret of their success.

If you're looking for an internal promotion then you already have access to the decision maker. If you're looking for an external role, you have to work a little harder. Social media networks such as LinkedIn are an excellent place to conduct research. The things that a business leader posts and shares will tell you what they value. The way that they describe their career history will tell you what they value in themselves, and consequently what others have given them recognition for, and consequently what they will look for in you.

Ultimately, your aim should be to get into a position where you can ask one very simple question:

"What is the secret to your success?" If you're developing your career within your current organisation, you have the opportunity to network with a wide range of leaders to identify their most valued personal qualities in this way. By definition, because they are senior managers, they have demonstrated the qualities that best align with the culture of the organisation, so you will likely find that they have many qualities in common with each other.

You might wonder how you can portray yourself as the right candidate to so many people, and the answer relates to the psychological principle of confirmation bias, in that people will only look for what they want to see. Almost anything that you do in excess of the quality they're looking for will go unnoticed, and therefore you can simply cover a range of qualities that you have discovered to be valuable, and they will focus on and remember the ones which they find valuable.

When we interviewed leaders to find out what they look for in a 'high potential', a list of qualities emerged which is realistically far too long for you to consider as a development guide. What is far more important is the correlation between how a leader sees him or her self and what they look for in a future leader. The list of qualities and their frequency in our wider survey is as follows.

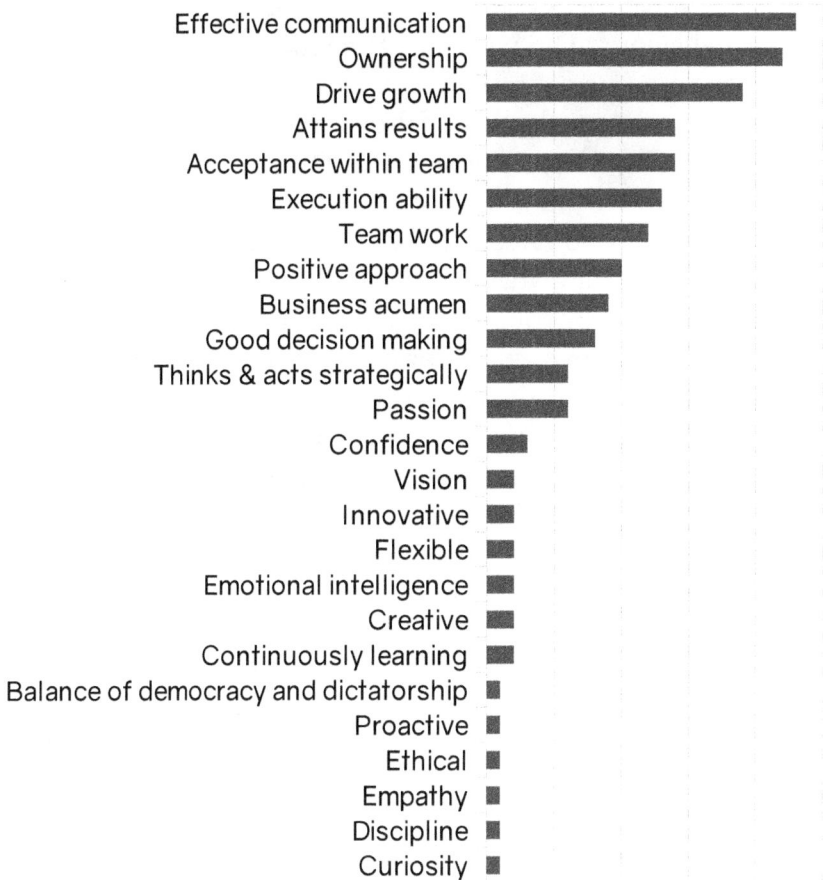

Quality	Frequency
Effective communication	████████████████
Ownership	███████████████
Drive growth	██████████████
Attains results	███████████
Acceptance within team	████████████
Execution ability	████████████
Team work	███████████
Positive approach	█████████
Business acumen	█████████
Good decision making	████████
Thinks & acts strategically	██████
Passion	██████
Confidence	███
Vision	██
Innovative	██
Flexible	██
Emotional intelligence	██
Creative	██
Continuously learning	██
Balance of democracy and dictatorship	█
Proactive	█
Ethical	█
Empathy	█
Discipline	█
Curiosity	█

If you're looking for some easy short cuts to developing your career, you'll look at the list and think that you can simply emulate those qualities in order to get ahead. That's not how it works, because smart leaders will see that you are not being true to yourself, they will see that you are putting on an act to impress them, and therefore they will know that your 'leadership behaviours' are neither consistent not credible.

Instead, what you must do is be yourself, do what you feel is right, focus on the things that are important to you, and focus on those valuable qualities when you are communicating with leaders.

What the list can help you to do is to highlight clear deficiencies in your behaviour. The participant mentioned above who failed to engage in a social group was afraid to do so. It was a fair assessment on the part of the VP that the participant felt 'out of his depth'. Certainly, if you're promoted into a leadership position and you avoid talking to the people you're working with, you're unlikely to be effective because you will find it harder to form the relationships that are vital for your success. Where you identify such gaps in your own habits and behaviours, seek help with them. Ask for a coach or mentor who can help you to analyse and close those gaps. At the very least, demonstrating that you are actively working on a characteristic is often as good as having the characteristic, because decision makers can see that you are able to acknowledge your gap areas and put in place a plan to address them. No-one expects you to be a perfect fit for every quality required in a role, however if you are at least aware of those qualities and honest with yourself about how you compare, then your open attitude will usually be seen as a highly admirable quality. As much as successful people want to share their secrets, they also want to see that you are eager to learn from them.

You might consider the list of qualities in the chart above as an idea of the kinds of qualities that leaders will be looking for when making their recommendations, however we can't stress enough that what matters most is not the generic qualities but the specific qualities that are unique to the recommenders and decision makers who you're building relationships with. If you don't know what they recognise as 'high potential' then you won't get very far.

When you believe that you're demonstrating all the right behaviours, but your efforts go unnoticed, the result will be frustration for you.

However, when you fail to demonstrate the behaviours that a stakeholder expects of you, the result will be disappointment for them.

In order to secure opportunities to develop your career, you must demonstrate the right qualities and be observed by the stakeholders who have an influence on your career.

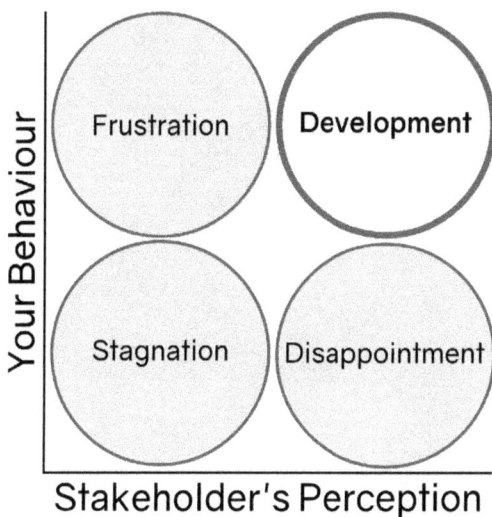

Only when these two factors of behaviour and perception are aligned will you achieve the career success that you seek.

The Second Glass Ceiling

Look back over your life. You have followed a path that has led you here, now. We have each followed a very different path in life, yet here we all are, together for this short time.

Take a blank piece of paper and consider a few times in your life where you felt that you were in exactly the right place, doing exactly what you were meant to do. Times when you felt a sense of purpose, a feeling that you were 'on track'.

Mark these events and their dates on a piece of paper like this:

These points will connect in a straight line:

Now consider times in your life when you felt like a square peg in a round hole, maybe times when you realised you were doing what someone else wanted, but it was absolutely wrong for you. Times when you felt a sense of being out of place, a feeling that you were "off track".

Mark these events and their dates on your piece of paper, thinking about which side of the line to place the mark, and how far away from the line, to represent how far you felt 'off course':

What does this tell you?

Organisations invest significant time and money in trying to work out who has potential. Talent management and succession programs evaluate and assess leadership candidates to try and figure out who might be 'leadership material'. And, time and again, all of the psychometric evaluations, leadership reviews and assessment centres fail to accurately predict a person's potential.

The paradox is that potential, by definition, is a capability to do something that you've never done before. Trying to predict how a person might behave in a future scenario is difficult at best because until that person is in the real scenario, they will not truly draw upon their capabilities. The toughest of people panic in situations of fairly low stress, and nervy, uncertain people become pillars of strength when faced with a challenge.

Time and again, 'high potential' candidates fail at the interview, and external recruits are hired instead, while staff who are temporarily seconded into management positions shine in ways that no-one predicted.

An added problem of talent management programs is that the assessment of who has 'potential' is largely subjective, and therefore that potential is not in any behaviour of the candidate, it is in the eye of the beholder, the perception and prejudice of the manager who is making the assessment. Potential is not something that you do, it is what someone else imagines you might do.

What we must therefore do is assess not potential but performance.

Finding your fear

Every time you put off a decision, or a phone call, or a task, you are being driven by fear. Fear of conflict, of being judged, of being criticised, of not being good enough and so on. These fears are normal, we learn them as children, and they affect us throughout our lives.

What are you afraid of? What is holding you back? Think about your first day in a new job or the first day you arrived at business school. When you met your colleagues, you were trying to prove something. You got up that morning and chose what to wear in order to create the 'right' impression. Professional? Laid back? Approachable? Unapproachable? You dressed and acted in order to prove something.

You went to great lengths to prove that you were not afraid.

If you're afraid of rejection, you set out to prove that you're likeable. If you're afraid of confrontation, you set out to prove that you're agreeable. If you're afraid of looking stupid, you set out to prove how smart you are. Even your chosen laptop and mobile phone prove something about you.

Amazingly, everyone can see through your pretence, they are fully aware of your fears. So why does nobody mention anything? Because they don't care. They're all too busy worrying about their own problems, and if they started pointing out yours, they risk exposing their own.

Your fear is therefore easy to identify – it's the aspect of you that you're trying to disprove.

- When you use jargon to prove you're smart, you're trying to disprove that you're stupid

- When you put others down to prove you're superior, you're trying to disprove that you're inferior

- When you display designer brands to prove you're valuable, you're trying to disprove that you're worthless

Of course, this doesn't mean that everyone who wears designer labels is afraid of being worthless, what's important is how you carry those labels.

A prominent trainer in the UK personal development market would begin his training sessions by slowly taking off his jacket and laying it on the stool behind him. He would make a show of folding his jacket inside out and placing it with the Armani label facing towards the audience.

Wearing a designer jacket is a very different behaviour to deliberately showing people that you've bought a designer jacket.

The irony is that everyone around you can see this; they can see through your pretence, your projection. They can see your fears and they can see your true nature. Why don't they say anything about it? Simply because they don't care. They have enough problems of their own to worry about yours. Besides, if they start drawing attention to your pretence, they risk being challenged on their own, so they prefer to keep quiet. We see the truth in others and keep quiet, they are doing the same with us.

The question we're left with is this: What are you trying to prove? And what is that telling people about you?

Common to every culture is the problem of self-worth. Throughout a person's career, they have been rewarded for certain behaviours, such as problem solving, technical knowledge, networking, relationship-building, even bullying. The person associates their sense of self worth with those rewards, and they become locked in a cycle of those behaviours. Unfortunately the qualities that got them this far will not get them to the next level, so they face the toughest challenge of all – to risk letting go of the qualities they most value in themselves.

When you look back through the 'life path' that you drew earlier, do you see a connection between those memorable moments in your life and your sense of self-worth?

Have you ever been in a situation where you were encouraged to behave in a certain way, and then after some time, criticised for exactly that? Did it feel unfair? Did you feel undermined? Even insecure?

Self-help gurus keep telling us that we must be independent, not reliant on feedback from others, not attached to what others think or feel about us. We must find our own path in life, we must be ourselves. What they can't tell us is how to figure out who we really are. One day, you just wake up and find yourself. You just don't know which day that will be, or where to look.

All of this talk about finding yourself and being your own person is, of course, misleading. We are a social species, evolved to function in groups and to experience depression and anxiety when alone. We are pre-programmed to avoid anything which would exclude us from a social group, so our fears of rejection, or abandonment, loss, conflict, punishment and so on are a very real and very important factor in our social behaviour, as is our need for status – not necessarily to have high status, but to know our status in a group.

All of our titles are relational. You might call yourself father, mother, son, daughter, brother, sister, consultant, head of HR, salesperson, leader, manager or recruiter. All of these titles do not define you, they define your relationship with others. If you want to know who you really are, look at the relationships which you have built around you.

We behave in order to 'fit in', and so in our careers, we behave in order to fit in with a working culture, and that culture, or the authority figures in that culture, reward us for those behaviours, so we carry on along that path, even though it isn't the one that's right. We only know that our path even exists when we're so far off it that we feel that sense of conflict and dissatisfaction.

Barriers to your career development are not imposed by your organisation, they are created by you. You are the only person holding yourself back. The second glass ceiling is your creation.

Your need to fit in causes you to behave in certain ways in order to win approval. Over time, you become genuinely good at certain things. I've coached a senior manager who enjoys tackling complex projects such as large scale technical integrations, business mergers and so on. But his capability in such projects is a by-product of something else – his need to isolate himself in order to avoid confrontation with people who might be displeased with him. Locking himself in his office to work on a proposal or read a contract is a perfect cover story. Isolating yourself is a natural reaction to a threat, but in reality he is not being threatened. His past experiences in life make him expect confrontation, and in avoiding contact, he causes conflict by introducing delays into business activities that depend on relationships.

The nature of your brain is such that you will become good at anything that you practice. You can't not. And if you practice failure, you'll become good at that too.

The second glass ceiling is very common with technical managers. Their skills in product design, or software, or law, or accounting principles mean that they get promoted to a first level management position, where their technical skills allow them to manage a group of technical people. This is partly based on the idea that if you don't know what your team are talking about, they must be lying to you.

The technician has been rewarded throughout their career for their technical skills, so they have created an implicit link between those skills and their own self worth. When a technician seems to get disproportionately agitated during a technical debate, this is why. By questioning their technical knowledge, you are questioning their self worth. It would be like someone telling you that you are worthless, useless, undesirable.

The technician therefore stays in their comfort zone and gets stuck at an organisational level where they can have their self worth boosted by technical tasks.

The biggest problem with being a technician is this: you *are* one.

Whatever you currently know becomes your area of expertise. It doesn't have to be overtly technical, it's the connection between knowledge and self worth that's the problem. You might be a software engineer, a leadership guru, a doctor or a lawyer, or you might just be the only person in the office who knows how to work the new coffee machine.

Anything that you do to progress on from this level makes you feel uncertain, insecure, even frightened. Within months of a promotion, you'll have retreated into your comfort zone, and you'll be doing the job of people 'beneath' you because that's what makes you feel good about yourself. You'll be 'helping' your team, working on their projects and totally undermining them. They'll feel worthless and under-utilised, but at least you'll be happy.

After a few more months, your team's performance will drop and you'll start to get turnover in your team. You'll kid yourself that they just don't have the level of skill required, and you keep having to do their jobs for them. You'll hire replacements who have a lower level of skill and experience so that you can 'mentor' them, because you know best.

While all of this is happening, the world has moved on and your technical knowledge starts to become out of date. You begin to wish you had stayed in a technical job. You get moved into a 'special projects' role which is a demotion in all but job title and pay. But at least you feel safe again.

Old people are well known for their 'in the good old days' nostalgia, but the reality is, we're *all* stuck in the good old days. We all hold onto our pasts as a way of defining our futures.

We are held back by the things we value most about ourselves. To move on, we must let go.

Breaking through

At the first glass ceiling you'll find people who are very good at promoting themselves, but they don't actually do a very good job. Do you know anybody like this? They get to a point in their career where they're found out and that becomes their limit. Other people do a really really good job but they don't talk about it. Do you know anyone like that? They do a great job, but nobody knows, they don't get visibility, they don't get recognised, so that holds them back in their career.

The first glass ceiling is not the problem. You are not held back by culture or prejudice. You are held back in your career right now by your own behaviours and habits; all the things that you've been rewarded for throughout your career. Because you have been rewarded for certain behaviours, you have come to think of them as your own unique qualities. You think that what you've been rewarded for is what makes you special or valuable. Well, certainly doing what other people find valuable certainly makes you valuable to them, but they might not have the same life goals and aspirations as you. They might not want what you want. Your behaviours and capabilities are convenient for them, but that might not serve your long term interests.

How you define yourself, how you see yourself, becomes a limit because another characteristic of human beings is that we want to be seen as consistent.

This phenomena of consistency is important in building your reputation, but it is also used to manipulate you into making commitments which you would not make in isolation. For example, in psychology experiments, when people were asked to make small commitments, they were more likely to agree to larger commitments later on. Experts in the field of organisational change often say that people are resistant to change. Whether this is true or not, there's no doubt that you like things the way that you like them. You have a favourite colour, you like your tea and coffee 'just right' and your tastes in music and books change very slowly, if at all.

From a psychological perspective, one of the important stages of brain development that we all go through enables us to create abstract maps of reality. As a young child, you learn to navigate both your physical environment and your relationships with others. Your sense of basic safety and security is dependent on the consistent attention and behaviour of others. As a child, your development into a normal, well-balanced adult was based on your relationships with others. Imagine that you live alone. Imagine if you came home from work one evening to find that your front door had changed. As you walk into your home, imagine that your furniture has moved around. How do you feel? Curious? Uneasy? Nervous? Afraid?

This is normal. Your reality has changed by an unseen hand. Your mental map has failed you. You are lost.

Your existence depends on the world staying much the same from one day to the next. And other people rely on you staying the same too.

The phenomena of consistency means that recruiters tend to play safe. Think about the executive search consultant who said that he looks for a 'career trajectory', a straight line through a person's past achievements which indicates that they had a strategy, a grand plan for their career development. In reality, a plan is something that we make as we look back, as we tell a story which connects together the random opportunities which come our way. We tell that story to a recruiter and pretend that it was our plan, all along.

Your story will feature you as the hero, of course, and your superpowers will be your best qualities, guaranteed to solve any problem and overcome any obstacle. When the recruiter asks you about a challenge that you have overcome, your story will feature your creativity, or your practicality, or your resilience, or whatever quality got you over the highest mountain and through the deepest ravine.

What you think you're good at, what you value in yourself is the limit on your career. This is the second glass ceiling. To get past the second glass ceiling you have to leave behind the things you most value yourself for, the things that you've been rewarded for. There's a connection here, it's not just about what you think you're valuable for, you have been rewarded for these behaviours, and through that cycle of reward, you have come to believe that this is what makes you valuable.

In order to push through the second glass ceiling, you have to leave behind everything that you value most about yourself. It's not your fault; employers have created this dependency by explicitly and implicitly rewarding you for your technical knowledge. They have rewarded you just like you would reward a dog for performing a trick. "Sit!" and you get a treat. "Write code! File accounts! Hit sales target! Good boy! Clever girl!"

Once you can acknowledge how this connection has been created, you can begin to break it. You can begin by recognising the times in your working life when you did something beyond what you were contracted to do, maybe you did more than you wanted to. Maybe you worked extra hours or took on extra responsibility. What made you do that? What was the need in you that was served by your compliance?

That need is driven by fear.

Your inner fear is so powerful that you protect it, every day, and you've spent so long protecting it that you've forgotten that it's there. But every so often, when you respond to something much more aggressively than you should, or something affects you much more deeply than is reasonable, you get a reminder that the fear is there, deep within you.

We're not born this way, but it is something that we learn very quickly.

The Second Glass Ceiling

The rewards of our careers make us associate certain behaviours with a sense of self worth, so the more we engage in those behaviours, the better we feel about ourselves, and the more we insulate ourselves from that fear that I mentioned.

When we're pushed out of our comfort zones by external events such as a promotion or change in job function, we feel the pressure of that fear, guiding us back into the safety of social compliance.

Fitting in might feel safe and easy, but for us as civilised, evolved humans, it is at odds with our need to be special, to be unique, to create, to make a mark on the world, to be seen, to be known, to leave a legacy.

This is our fundamental contradiction. We want to fit in and stand out, at the same time.

In order for something to have worth, two things are necessary; a valuer, and a currency. Whether we measure value in Euros, or gold bars, or time saved, or aesthetic pleasure, we place a comparative value on everything and everyone in our lives. This is the paradox of the self-worth that the personal development gurus talk about – it's actually not possible to value yourself, because that would make you both the valuer and the object to be valued. You can be one or the other, not both.

In any society, we judge and are judged by others. That's not something to fear or reject, and in fact, people who reject judgement are simply trying to protect themselves from what they fear will be an unpleasant judgement. The person who says, "I don't care what other people think about me" cares very much. They just don't want to get hurt.

To break through your fears and explore outside of your comfort zone first means acknowledging those fears. You can't change what doesn't exist, so denying your fears only leaves you at risk of exploitation by others. Throughout history, con artists have been highly skilled at recognising people who deny their own weaknesses.

Our value is created in the minds of others, and therefore our sense of worth is dependent on feedback from others. When that feedback is, "You only got 99% in your exam? Why couldn't you have got 100%? I bet the kid next door got 100%", we learn that whatever we do isn't quite good enough. The problem is that for most things in life, there is no simple marking system, so we don't actually know what constitutes 100%. What would be a 100% job? What would be 100% of your potential? Who would be 100% the right partner for you? What would make your children 100%?

As a student, you take the test, you don't mark it. You don't rate your own performance. As an athlete, someone else holds the stopwatch. If you're always looking over your shoulder at the other competitors, your focus isn't on giving your best.

Breaking through the second glass ceiling isn't about being the best, and it isn't about being better than your competitors. It isn't even about being better than you were yesterday, because we cannot set out to improve anything – improvement is a measure, not a target. Even so, you try to improve things in your life every day.

Breaking through means being prepared to do something different and see what happens.

To improve or perfect something requires two things; a standard and a measure. You compare something that you're working on to a standard, and you make adjustments to minimise the differences. You can't ever recreate the standard exactly because your measurements will always contain errors. The standard will always be unique, as will your reproduction. However, you can recreate something close enough to the standard for the intended purpose.

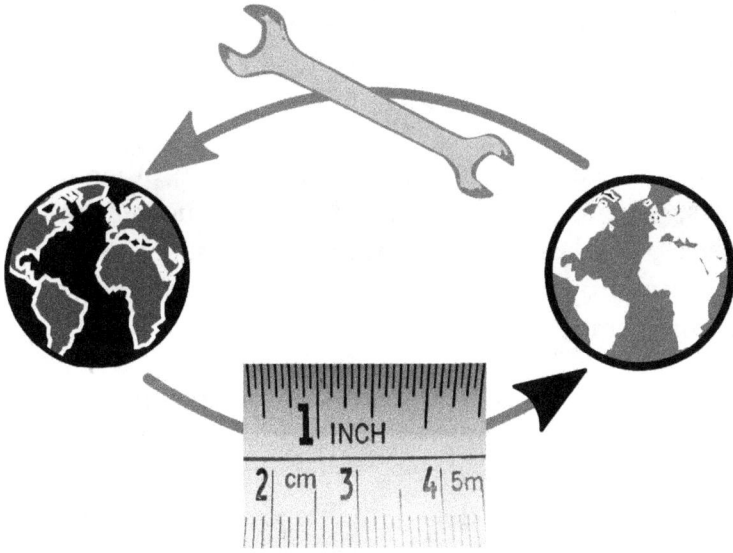

Many people try to be perfect. They set unrealistically high standards for themselves, but perfect is not an end state, it is a process. Those standards are not even their own, they are inherited from parents and teachers who regarded any achievement as being 'not good enough' without being specific about what 'good enough' means or how to measure it. This starts with judgements about academic performance and leads to judgements about career and life choices. "I just felt you could have done better", says the parent who wants more for their children.

You can only ever do what you do. Doing the *right* thing is a matter of perception, doing *something* is all that really counts. In reality, you can never have done better, you can only have done different. You have no way of knowing how that would have worked out.

Making changes is all that matters. Do those changes become improvements? We can only know that when we look back and measure the effects of those changes.

As humans we have the ability to predict the future, which is very important when we're crossing a busy road or catching a ball. However, we also try to predict what other people will do, which is dangerous because people are not simple physical objects without free will.

We are defined by our relationships with others. We are brothers, sisters, fathers, mothers, sons, daughters, managers, employees, coaches, clients, trainers, teachers, students. And yet being defined by those relationships cannot mean that we are limited by them.

As an adult, you know that feedback from others is not always honest, sometimes they have an agenda. Even your parents had an agenda – to protect you, to save you from the mistakes that they made, but in so doing, they recreate those mistakes in another generation. You can be constrained by that, or you can choose to break free and follow your own path, which ultimately is what parents want for their children anyway, they just want them to be safe at the same time. Fit in and stand out.

We assign our own worth based on feedback from others. We have to stay true to what we want for ourselves, and when we value ourselves, others will learn how to value us.

Look back at the path that you drew for yourself. When you take the 'on purpose' line and extend it forwards into the future, where does it lead you?

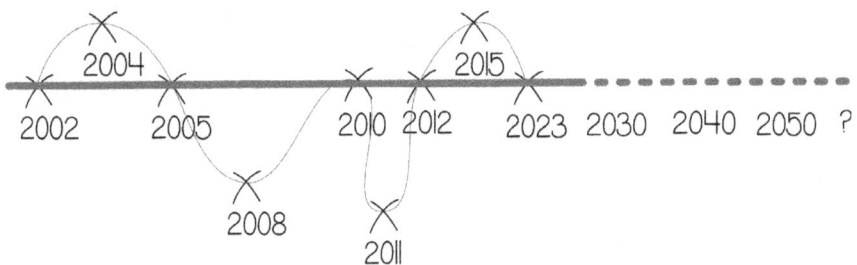

That's where you have to focus.

You're on a journey, and that journey has never been travelled before, by anyone. It is your path, it is unique, you are unique. No-one has ever lived your life before, made your mistakes

The Second Glass Ceiling

before, learned your lessons before. We learn nothing from success in life, we only learn from failure, because success only teaches you to carry on doing what you're doing. Failure teaches you that there was more to do, more to think about, that the world wasn't exactly the way you thought it was. Success doesn't come from having perfect plans, it comes from being open to feedback and making changes, fast. Success doesn't come from prediction, it comes from adaptation.

Take a few minutes to try this exercise. Take a piece of paper and write down what you feel is your most valuable career skill, the quality or trait which you believe is your own personal secret for success. Take a moment to physically write that down.

Take a few moments to read what you have written. Consider what it means to you, think about times when you have been free to express this, times when you have been rewarded for it, and times when, if you're honest with yourself, you have also been exploited.

Now hold the piece of paper carefully and study it…

…and tear it up. Screw it into a ball and throw it away.

On a fresh, new sheet of paper, write down what you want to be valued for in the future.

Getting through the second glass ceiling means that you have to take a risk, and it's possibly the greatest risk of your life. You have to let go of the things you most value about yourself – your history, your knowledge, your skills, all of the things that you have been rewarded for throughout your life. When you let go of everything that you were, you risk walking an unknown path, running off the edge of the map. The past is safe, but it's also limiting.

When you let go of what you were, you can become more than you ever imagined.

The Career Cycle

Career planning is important, however most people's career plans are made looking backwards, not forwards. As you move through your career, many of the moves you make arise through chance, opportunity, networking and so on. New positions and ideas are suggested to you, and new roles are continually created that you could not have planned for. Therefore, the reality of your career path is a combination of strategy and opportunity.

As you look back along your career path, you might notice that your career steps tend to follow a consistent pattern. Parts of that pattern are obvious, others less so. For example, you might go for an interview before being offered a new position, and you might also work on succession planning, even if you're not in a leadership role, to ensure a smooth handover of whatever work you're leaving behind.

If you focus only on what you want, the roles and activities that interest you, and on what others can do to support your career development, you will most likely be frustrated that your career isn't progressing as you would wish. Much of your focus needs to be on reputation management, and that is based on what you are willing to give, not what you want to take.

Take a look at the following diagram of the career cycle. This was developed by interviewing a range of people across different industries who demonstrated consistent skill in managing their own career development rather than waiting to be given their next promotion. We live in an increasingly noisy world, in which you can no longer afford to wait to be recognised and rewarded, because other people are doing the same job as you, to the same high standard. You have to be good at your job, and you have to be good at marketing too.

In the following diagram, you'll see a cycle of steps. Identify the step that best describes where you currently are in your career.

Identify role models and influencers

Create succession plan for current role

Identify target roles

Map organisational structure and roles

Identify values and long term aspirations

Understand current skills and capabilities

Start new role

Close any skills gaps

Position and influence

Create a new role if none already exists

Seek shadowing and secondment opportunities

Formal application process

Interview coaching and practice

Implement succession plan for current role

Ongoing:

Communicate with current line manager

Set & measure short term goals

Build & maintain network

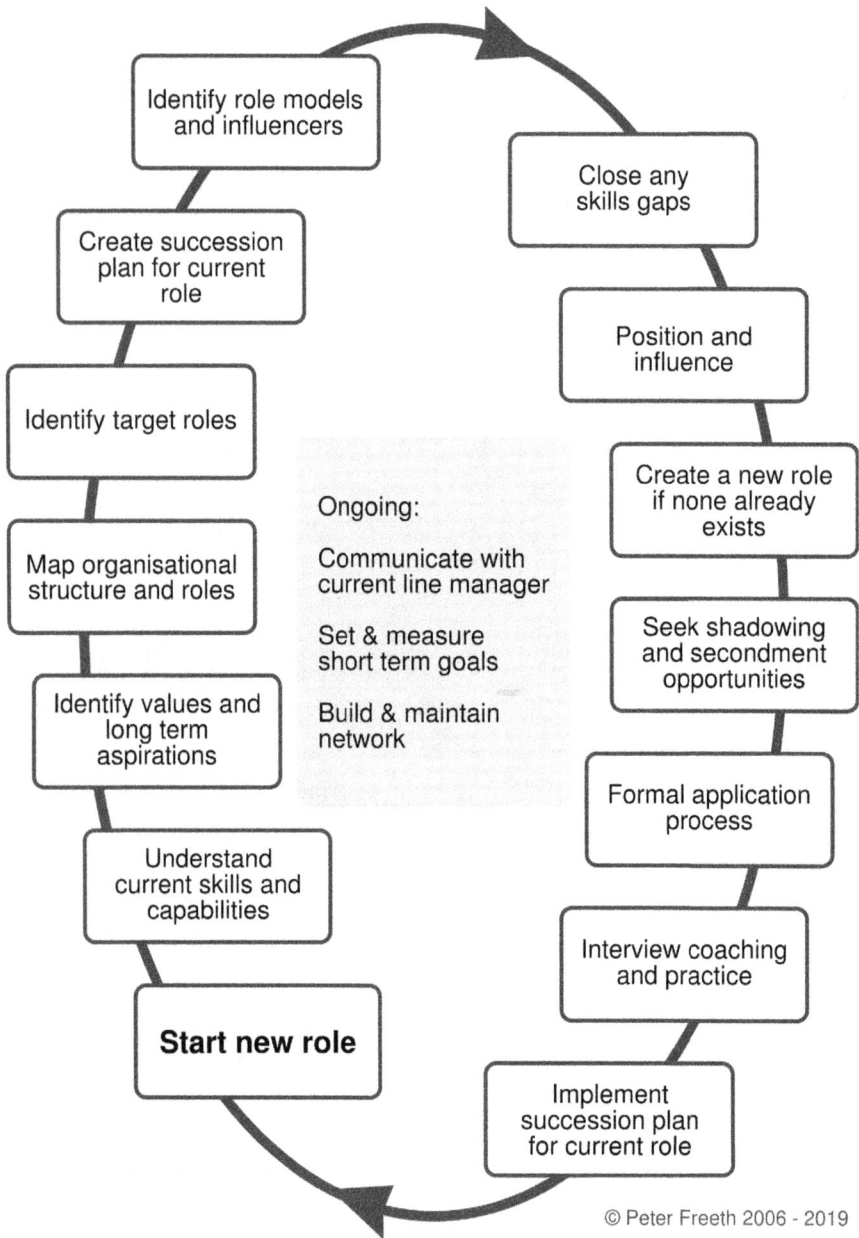

© Peter Freeth 2006 - 2019

If, for example, you are currently thinking about your next role, you would be at the 'Identify target roles' step. That would mean that you're wasting your time trying to 'Position and influence' with stakeholders because that step is too far away from where you currently are. If you don't know what your next step is, you don't know who to network with, and your networking activities can then be either unfocused, or worse, perceived as politically motivated.

In this example, the best you can do is to start identifying potential stakeholders and to create your succession plan. Moving on from your current role is inevitable, so you will need a successor, even though you don't yet know which direction you'll move in.

If you're planning a move within your present organisation, succession planning is critical. Firstly, your successor will push you into your next role. Secondly, having a successor will mean you can make a clean role and not end up straddling two roles until a replacement is found.

If you're currently a manager of a team, succession planning doesn't mean identifying a single named successor, because that person's career plans are not under your control, and to identify only one person exposes you to a number of risks:

- Your one successor might have other plans and let you down

- When your other team members know they're not considered as successors, they will become demotivated and your performance will suffer

- Your choice of successor is likely based on subjective bias rather than actual performance

- You miss the opportunity to see if other members of your team had potential that you had not previously recognised

The approach to succession planning that we would therefore recommend is to begin delegating all of your management responsibilities to your team on a rotation basis. This allows you to give everyone a fair and equal chance of development and assessment. You can see two factors which are very important; first, who is willing to rise to the challenge and two, who is able.

Often, managers judge capability based on willingness to volunteer, and this has a tendency to lead to political empire-building and recognition for supporting the manager. One of the most vital factors of team culture that any manager can encourage is that of constructive conflict. If the whole team agrees with everything the manager says, that's a sure sign of organisational politics which is at odds with organisational performance.

Navigating the Career Cycle

Using the career cycle map, identify where you are right now.

Look at the next step and make a list of some activities which you can focus on in the short term.

You might even plan some of those activities into your diary to help maintain your focus on building momentum.

Unfortunately, your career does not progress in neat steps. Sometimes, you move into a role before you're ready, because the role unexpectedly becomes available and you're the only candidate. Sometimes, a move is long overdue, and follows a period of stagnation through lack of development until a suitable role becomes available. Sometimes, you will limit your options by choosing to stay with your current employer, or in your current geographic area.

Some organisations take these factors into account when considering who is a 'high potential'. Dr Elliot Jacques, a Canadian psychologist, created the Requisite Organization Model which includes, amongst other things, a way of identifying the right people for roles in an organisation by assessing a candidate against four criteria. The purpose is twofold; to find a person who is a good match for a role, and to find a role which will make the candidate feel happy and fulfilled in their work.

The four criteria are as follows.

- SKEE (Skills, Knowledge, Education, Experience)

- IPC (Information Procession Capability)

- Temperament

- Accepts Role Requirements

SKEE contains elements which are perhaps easy to develop through training and seeking out new experiences.

IPC is not just about how smart a person is, but also includes their ability to make complex decisions, to make sense of the available data and the level of detail that they are comfortable with in order to make a decision and take action.

Temperament is important because poor alignment of a person's temperament with the reality of the job can lead to a high level of challenge, resulting in burnout, or a low level of challenge, resulting in boredom and disengagement.

Accepts Role Requirements is an interesting point to consider. For example, a role might be based in a regional headquarters, requiring that you relocate. Your family may or may not be open to this idea, based on their age, the location in question and so on. If your career shareholders can't support your move into the role, there's no point pursuing it because without their investment, you're unlikely to succeed. By identifying that early into your journey, you will save yourself a great deal of time and stress later on.

An option which is always available to you is to create a new role where one does not already exist. Most people tend to focus on existing hierarchies and roles, fitting themselves into a limited selection of boxes and trying to position themselves to fit a role profile which was written long ago, and probably for someone else. This suggests a further problem with existing roles – in order for you to be selected, someone else has vacated that role, leaving a shadow that hangs over you. Your predecessor has created a set of unique working relationships around them, and you have to work hard to reset the expectations of stakeholders.

Experts disagree on how many new roles will be created in the future. A report from IT company Dell predicts that '85% of jobs that will exist in 2030 haven't been invented yet', while a BBC investigation puts the figure closer to a third. Predictions from futurologists are notoriously unreliable, yet we only have to look at an online job board to see that in 2023, there are indeed jobs available which did not exist a decade ago. This contributes to the shrinkage of the career island that you're perched on, and it also presents an excellent opportunity for you.

Organisational design always lags behind organisational demand. People will fill in gaps, expand their roles, create new knowledge and new systems, all to meet ever-changing customer behaviour. Someone will see that something needs doing which is nobody's specific role, and they will do it, because they are focused on how they can deliver the corporate mission, rather than saying, "It's not my job" and leaving it to someone else. At some later point in time, the activity, and the area of responsibility, becomes someone else's official job, and a new role, or even a new team, is created.

You have the opportunity to pre-empt this process by being aware of gaps in the organisation's capability to achieve its goals, and creating proposals for a new role, crafted around your own skills and interests.

As we have already mentioned, there are jobs today which did not exist a decade ago, and we have even seen new roles created within the lifespan of a single talent management program. In other words, we have seen people successfully creating new roles which did not previously exist, in order to meet an operational need which was not being effectively met.

This approach absolutely depends on having a strong network, and having the ability to think strategically, because the success of your business case depends on well researched, accurate and compelling data.

There are two types of situation where you might take this approach. The first is that you can see the needs of customers have evolved, and the organisation is attempting to meet those needs but in a way which stretches existing resources, resulting in a poor quality of service in multiple areas. For example, a new sales strategy might lead to increased customer service calls, and the customer service team might be responding to these, but they lack the technical knowledge and relationships to do so effectively. Not only are the new calls not handled effectively, the increased workload also results in service quality for existing customers being affected.

We might call this a 'remedial' opportunity, in which a change of organisational structure would solve a problem. The second type of opportunity looks to future potential, and we might call it a 'generative' opportunity, because there is no existing template or expectation to build upon, we must generate something new.

Each type of opportunity presents its challenges. The most common objection to the remedial opportunity is for budget holders to say, "But it's fine right now, it will work itself out, we don't need to spend any money". The generative opportunity presents the risk of the unknown. What if your plan doesn't work out? What if it doesn't lead to extra revenue?

You might recognise both of these objections as being based on fear, and you will already know that the way to overcome this is to build trust. Whether you're moving to an existing role or creating a new one, that fear of the unknown is always the issue that you can work to overcome by networking and building trust.

Organisations redesign and restructure on a regular basis in order to adapt to change. You can either wait for that to happen in the hope that an attractive role will become available, or you can stay one step ahead and build a case for a role which you believe will add measurable value in the future.

Your career progress should not be limited by job titles. As we have already said, your skills and experience don't progress in neat steps which coincide with the roles that you occupy.

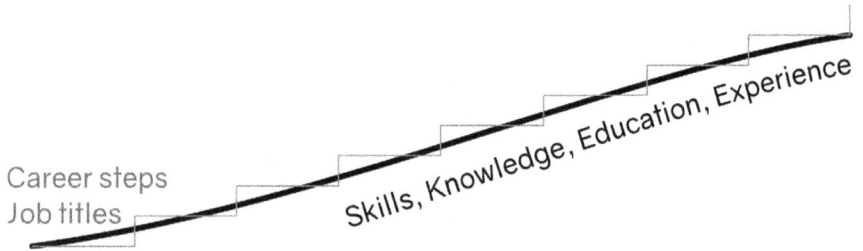

Career steps
Job titles

Skills, Knowledge, Education, Experience

Sometimes, your capabilities exceed what is required in a role, and sometimes you will feel out of depth as you catch up with the demands placed upon you. The times when you feel perfectly suited to your role will realistically be very infrequent, as your career trajectory takes you through successively more complex or challenging roles.

A 'high potential' doesn't wait to be discovered. You must demonstrate your potential by driving forward your career development and creating new opportunities, even when none exist today.

To paraphrase the great military leader Hannibal, either find a way, or make one.

Profiling the Decision Maker

As we have said, your next career move depends on a decision maker or key influencer seeing your potential and aligning that with their own values. The major problem that this creates for you is – how do you know their values?

If you have regular direct access to the decision maker, you can observe them, and you can ask them. There are some very simple questions that you can ask, and we will share those with you shortly.

A more common situation is that you are in a different office to the decision maker, or even a different country. How can you hope to influence them, when you have no opportunity to meet them, and your only interaction is indirect through other people, or direct via conference calls and low quality video links?

The answer, if you are lucky, is surprisingly simple.

The decision makers who are most likely to support your career growth are also focused on their own career trajectory, and that means that they have to actively engage in PR in order to create future opportunities for themselves. That PR tells you everything you need to know. PR, or Public Relations, encompasses marketing, advertising, anything to manage public perception.

Here are some examples from one of our LinkedIn contacts. What do you think this person is trying to tell you?

> "Enjoyed doing this talk in [city] last week. Having turned from hunter to hunted, it's been educational to see the approaches agencies and other B2B organisations use to gain attention. The pity is they are often poorly thought though and executed."

> "Sharing some thoughts on how to increase your hit and retention rates over dinner, we all cringed a bit at the things we've all done which haven't produced results, yet also acknowledged when good practice works and lessons learned."

"Thanks for the mention, glad you enjoyed the talk today and happy you've a few things to take away and implement."

"Last night I was invited to do an after dinner talk to a roomful of creative agencies, giving them a buyer's perspective of what things we look for, what works, what doesn't."

"Gaining attention in a world where senior execs are time prioritised is becoming more difficult."

"In a B2B environment, the battle for attention will often only be won with relevancy and personalisation when going in cold. Research will pay you a big dividend, using the right approach, identifying the right stakeholders and helping to solve pain points or support strategic intent give you a fighting chance of getting closer to the door."

Casual reading of this person's LinkedIn posts reveals that the majority contain references to public speaking and giving advice, with some references to his status. This is good to know, because you can see the qualities that this person values. The challenge, in this example, is the preference for giving advice. If this person were to interview you, and you also liked giving advice, you could create conflict which would not leave the best impression. Instead, this quality would perhaps best be matched by the desire to learn from others. If you were to ask this person for his advice on various subjects, you could probably get him talking for a very long time, and he would likely feel very good about that.

If you see no obvious PR opportunity, and no obvious clues in the decision maker's communication, and if they have been in their current role for many years, then this also tells you all you need to know.

What we will do is learn how to map the decision maker's internal perceptions and experiences by observing their external behaviour and communication.

Whilst we communicate for a number of different reasons, the fundamental driver behind communication in any social animal is to increase our chances of survival. Communication takes a lot of energy, and we are very energy-efficient animals, so we only communicate what and when we really need to. Therefore, everything that any person says to you is said for a very simple and very important reason – it's because that's what they want you to know.

This simple fact is very easy to miss. When a colleague tells you that they're busy, or stressed, you have to ask yourself why they want you to know that.

Every word spoken or written by any person is, by definition, what they choose to say, and it is not the whole story.

When your colleague tells you that they feel stressed, what are they missing out? What are they not telling you?

We're sure you've had the experience of a colleague or friend telling you half of the story, the half that favours them, or the half that gets you to do what they want. There is always more to the story.

When you write your CV or profile or résumé, you don't include everything that happened, you edit your life story in order to project a certain image. What you don't realise is that the image you explicitly describe in the summary is often different to the image conveyed by the rest of the document. You give away the real truth in the structure of what you say, and whether the reader is technically skilled in interpreting that structure or not, we all have an innate sense of language that gives us the feeling that 'they're not telling me everything'.

You have to realise that if you're telling only the best parts of the story, then so is everyone else. The important point for us is this: how do you know which are the 'best' parts? Simply, the parts of your story that you emphasise are what you want other people to know about you. This is how we will discover the values and preferences of the decision makers who will enable your career growth.

Most professionals have a social media profile, especially if they want to maximise their career options. The next chart shows the number of LinkedIn users in various countries, in millions of users.

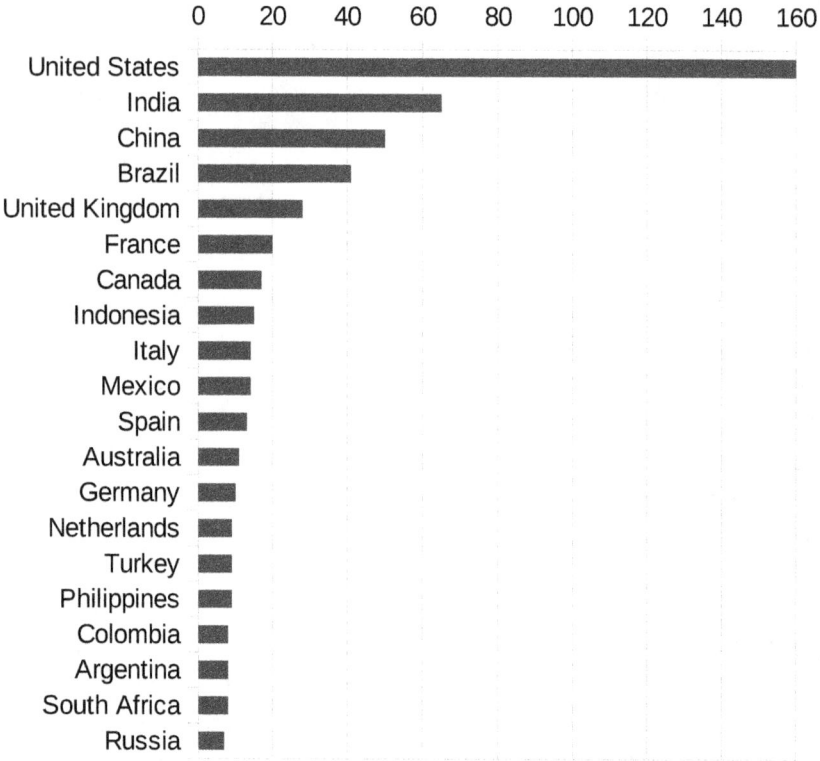

Source: Statista, 2020

If we look instead at the percentage usage of LinkedIn compared to each country's population then we can see how likely you are to find your target decision makers on LinkedIn in each country:

Profiling the Decision Maker

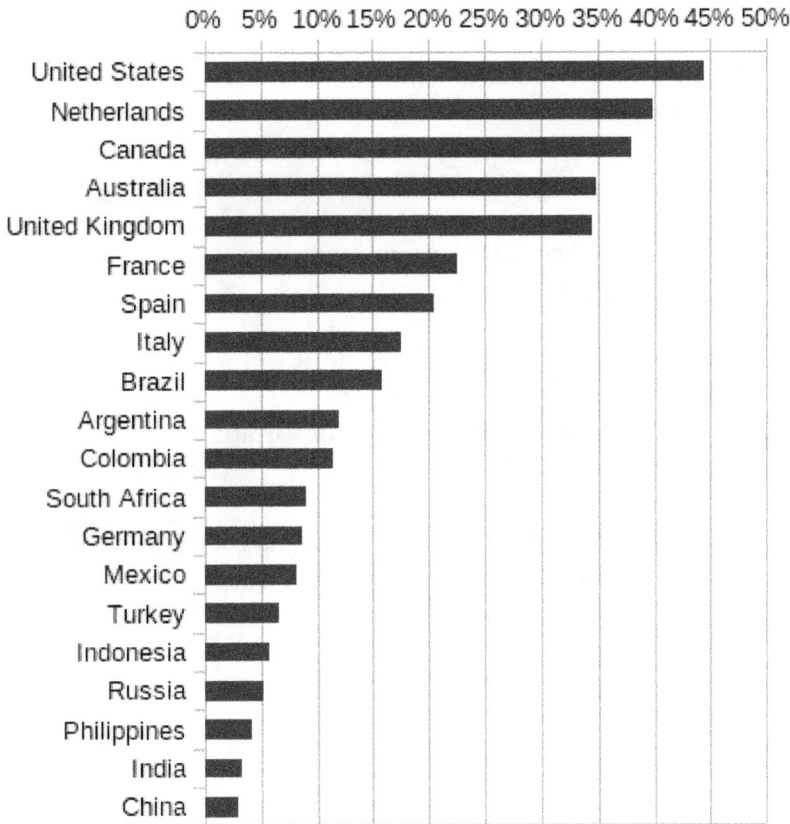

	0%	5%	10%	15%	20%	25%	30%	35%	40%	45%	50%

United States
Netherlands
Canada
Australia
United Kingdom
France
Spain
Italy
Brazil
Argentina
Colombia
South Africa
Germany
Mexico
Turkey
Indonesia
Russia
Philippines
India
China

Source: Statista, 2020

In many Asian countries, Facebook is much more popular for business use. As of 2020, Facebook has around 2.6 billion active users worldwide, whilst LinkedIn has around 675 million.

Whatever the platform, remember the golden rule; that your target decision maker will not be sharing their 'real selves' via social media, they will be sharing what they want their peers, and other influencers, to see. This in turn reveals exactly what you need to know – the qualities which they admire in themselves, and which they will therefore seek out in future leaders.

We promised to share some questions that you can ask if you have direct access to your target decision maker. They're very simple, and you can probably guess what they are:

- What is the secret of your success?

- What are the qualities that got you to where you are today?

- What advice would you give me for success in my career?

- What advice would you give anyone to help them reach their full potential?

- What are the qualities that you look for in a future leader?

- What do you think is the most important action for a new leader to focus on?

The purpose here is not to bombard your target with all of these questions. Just ask one and then listen, very carefully.

Breaking Through the Noise Barrier

In one minute on the internet more that three million items are shared on Facebook, nearly one million swipes on Tinder, 139,000 hours of video are watched on YouTube, 69,500 hours of video are watched on Netflix, 95,000 apps are downloaded from the Google play store, 100 new website domains are registered. The problem with networking is that everybody is doing it. You do a great job but so does everybody else. That noise creates a barrier that you have to break through.

You make decisions every day, about what car to buy, what to have for lunch, where to invest your savings, which projects to focus on. While you're gathering information to make the right decisions, other people are trying to influence you. Advertisers make everything sound wonderful, and some industries even create confusion to force you to turn to their advisers for help.

You're probably the kind of person who feels it's important to weigh up all of the information before you make the right decision, and when you make the right decision that you feel good about, you tend to stay with it because being weak and indecisive is not a desirable quality that you would recognise in yourself. Maybe you have doubts about the right choice, but in the long run you know that making commitments and sticking to them keeps you on the right path. You are consistent and reliable. You're a morally driven person who always aims to do the right thing.

Let's try an experiment. Choose one of these envelopes:

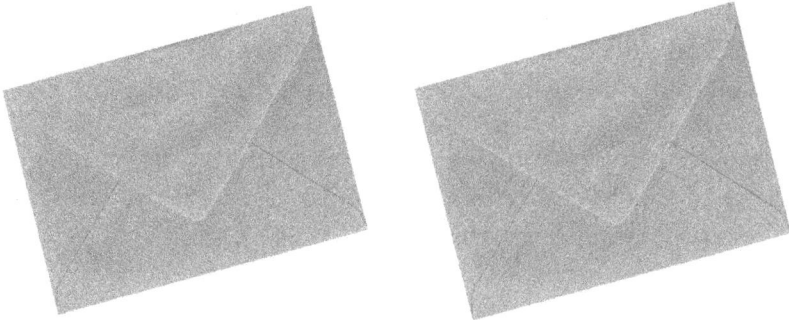

Remember your choice and we'll come back to it later on.

You might feel that shouting about your achievements is not the right way to develop your career. Perhaps, as a child, you were told not to brag or make yourself more important than others. Perhaps you feel that people who shout about their own achievements are being political, and you don't want to be seen as a political player.

Your dilemma is that your competitors are indeed shouting about their achievements, and if you don't join in, you'll be left behind. You're stuck. You don't want to brag, and you don't want to be overtaken by your competitors.

Here's the challenge – how to be heard above the background noise without compromising your ethical standards.

If you go to any market in a tourist area, you'll hear salespeople trying their best to overcome this problem. "Nice nice!" "Good price" "Hey!" "Come look!" Very quickly, you adapt to the onslaught of invitations to view a wide range of high quality merchandise and you learn first to say "no" and then to ignore the shouting completely. You learn to tune out the noise.

You might think that, in broadcasting your achievements, this puts you at a disadvantage because recruiters will tune out all the shouts of "Hey! Nice candidate here!" "Look at me!" and "I'm the best candidate, look at my long list of achievements!"

In fact, this presents you with an advantage for the simple reason that shouting loudest is not the way to cut through background noise. By far the best way to cut through noise is to be more specific and selective. Identify your target and communicate in a way which slips right through your competitors' noise.

In practice, this means that broadcasting your message is counter-productive, because it simply adds to the noise that you're trying to cut through.

By the way, remember which envelope you decided on. Do you want to change or hold on to the one you chose? It's important.

What you therefore have to do is identify the roles you're most interested in, then work out how to position yourself as a low risk candidate for those roles. You then have to identify the decision makers and make direct contact with them, making your communication as concise and direct as possible. Simple!

If it's so simple, why isn't everyone doing it? For the same reason that you're not doing it. You're afraid that if you target your message and you 'miss', you've wasted your opportunity and ruined your chances. So you do what everyone does, you hedge your bets, cast your net wide and hope for the best. You do this because you are afraid of rejection.

You worry that if you identify one perfect role, and one decision maker, and you alienate that one person, you have lost your only chance. As a result of this, you approach tentatively, perhaps indirectly, hoping to be noticed. You may well be noticed, but not for being a strong candidate for the role. You'll be noticed for lacking in the confidence required to go out and get what you want. You'll be noticed as the person who loiters around at the back of the room, hiding in the shadows, waiting to be discovered. The problem is that no-one is looking for you. There are no talent scouts on the lookout for new leaders, because there are more than enough people at the front of the queue.

Think of the leader who noticed the high potential candidate at the networking events, appearing disengaged, holding back. He was noticed, but not as a future leader. If you are selected for a talent or development program, you are being noticed.

Also think about the retail manager who targetted local businesses who were not current customers. She did something that her competitors were not doing. For you to do the same means that you have to know what your competitors are doing. You have to learn the system and work out how everyone else is using it, and then you have to use it differently.

For example, let's say that there's a formal reporting system for whatever KPI our job entails; perhaps for sales figures, production data, customer satisfaction and so on. Everyone is using the same system, so the only way for you to get noticed is to deliver a result that stands head and shoulders above the results of your colleagues. This means that, in order to cut through the noise, you have to have the loudest voice in the room. And that in turns means that you have to work a lot harder, and be a lot smarter, than everyone else. Realistically, that's very unlikely to happen because targets are set at a certain level for a reason.

A normal distribution of performance will mean that the majority of people will perform at an average level, and only a small minority will stand above the rest. The amount of work you have to put in to achieve such notable results is extremely time-consuming. Of course, you always have the option to lie about your results, which will get short term attention for the right reasons, and long term attention for the wrong reasons.

We know of a talent program participant who was highly motivated to be the best salesperson in his region, and this was driven by a deeper motivation to win his parents' approval. However, when his luck ran out and the regional economy slowed down, his success came under threat. Since delivering sales results in a challenging economic climate is hard work, he fabricated his results. For a while, this worked out very well. He looked good, his boss looked good, and his boss' boss looked good. All of this was based on promises which were never fulfilled. When the extent of his illusion came to light, he was invited to reconsider his career options. Of course, his colleagues and bosses must have known that something wasn't right, but it suited them to turn a blind eye. This is exactly the kind of delusional thinking that got Volkswagen into such trouble with the emissions scandal of 2015. His LinkedIn profile now reads, "A highly reliable professional business advisor. Repeated success of exceeding sales & revenue targets. Often demonstrate exceptional judgment and takes appropriate actions."

A story like this is embarrassing to leaders, so when they did begin to suspect, it was too late for them to avoid being caught up in the scandal, and so it is generally better to let the situation continue in the hope that either no-one finds out, or that they can blame it all on a scapegoat, which is exactly what Volkswagen did, and is also what UBS did in 2012. According to the BBC, "A City trader who lost £1.4bn ($2.2bn) of Swiss bank UBS's money has been jailed for seven years after being found guilty of two counts of fraud. Southwark Crown Court heard Kweku Adoboli was 'a gamble or two away from destroying Switzerland's largest bank'. He lost the money in 'unprotected, unhedged, incautious and reckless' trades, the jury was told. He had denied the charges, which related to the period between October 2008 and September 2011."

Those reckless trades would have made UBS a lot of money at the time, and would have made him, and his boss, and his boss's boss, look very good indeed.

At a UK telecoms operator back in the early 2000s, a specialist salesperson helpfully offered to complete order paperwork for account sales teams. The general account managers didn't understand the technicalities of the information they had to put on the paperwork and were very happy for him to take the problem off their hands. He then added his name to the paperwork, and was awarded the corresponding recognition for his sales results. He was the highest performing and highest paid salesperson in the team, and almost never left his house, except for team meetings and celebrations. His story is only tempered by what he did with his bonus payments – he used them to fund charity and community support projects in India.

Therefore, we can rule out 'exceeding your targets' as a reliable way of getting noticed. It's hard work, and someone else can always create more noise than you by bending the rules.

Instead, you need to do what your colleagues aren't doing, you need to 'move the goalposts'. Intellectually, you know it's good to do something different, the problem is working out what to do that will actually make the right difference. Fortunately, that's easy, and the clues are right in front of you.

Although you have targets to hit and formal KPIs to measure, you will also see the behaviours which are informally recognised, and those are the behaviours to focus on. What does your manager focus on during team meetings? What are the actions that are recognised by other leaders? These clues tell you the real KPIs which you can focus on in order to cut through the noise.

Which envelope did you choose at the start of this chapter? If you chose the 'right' envelope then sorry, it's not your lucky day. The $100 bill was in the 'left' envelope.

What factors influenced your decision? And how can you learn something from this experiment that will help you to build your career capital? Try the experiment again with your friends and colleagues and see what happens. Read them the text that comes before the image of the two envelopes, and give them the opportunity to change their choice if they wish. This centuries old 'trick' works because people are so preoccupied with being right that they don't notice how they are being influenced. It's worth discovering how you are being influenced on a daily basis, and therefore how you can turn this to your own advantage.

The Behaviours of High Potentials

We surveyed business leaders who are responsible for hiring decisions. We asked them to identify the traits that they look for in a 'high potential' candidate and we then condensed those traits into the following list. If you want to be recognised as a 'high potential', here are the behaviours that you need to exhibit:

- Attention to detail
- Team player, collaborative, build relationships
- Accountability, integrity
- Alignment, customer focus
- Open minded, approachable, good listener
- Business knowledge
- Strength, persistence, flexibility
- Delegate, develop your team
- Decisive, analytical
- Passionate
- Focus on goals, KPIs
- Fast to decide and act
- Creative
- Good communication
- Time management, multitasking
- Personal learning
- Cultural adaptation
- Healthy

You might be wondering why we didn't just give you the list at the start of the book. Well, that would make a very short book. Also, this list is useless to you.

First, for the reasons that we've already explained, demonstrating these behaviours is not enough. The right people have to notice you, and you have to stand out from your competitors.

Second, there are simply too many behaviours for you to focus on, and without focus, you're just part of the background noise.

Third, these are not behaviours. They are judgements.

From a technically linguistic point of view, these terms are 'lost performatives', words which look like actions, and take the place of an action in a statement, but which logically cannot be an action because other information is missing.

Let's take 'good communication' as an example. Who judges the quality of the communication? Thanks to our cognitive bias, we usually judge our own communication by what we think we said, and we judge other people's communication by what we think we heard. Good communication requires at least two people, and is still not an action. You can speak, but you cannot communicate. Communication is a judgement that you make after a period of time as you look back over a sequence of events. Since you've spent your whole life thinking of yourself as a good communicator, it can be a difficult concept to get your head around, so here's another example.

Think of someone who you love. What action is 'loving'? What exactly is it that you do in the process of loving? Perhaps you think of that person often, perhaps you send them messages, perhaps you remember their birthday, perhaps you do 'nice' things for them, perhaps you miss them when you are apart. If you were in a public place like a bar or restaurant, would you be able to recognise people who were in love, and people who were not? How would you recognise that difference?

The Behaviours of High Potentials

Throughout your life, you have experienced love; in relationships, by observing the relationships of your parents and family, in books and movies. You have come to form an abstract understanding of love, and that abstract concept is called, in technical linguistic terms, a 'complex equivalence'. Buying someone flowers does not mean that you love them. Sometimes, allowing someone to fail is an act of love, if you believe that the person will learn something valuable in the process. We might therefore say that love is an attitude or an intention, but it is not an action.

Running, sitting, speaking, standing, crying, watching – these are actions. When running turns into rushing, or fleeing, or chasing, we have added in extra information to form a judgement. 'Running' is a verb, whilst 'rushing' is a lost performative.

Our list of leadership qualities, derived from well over a hundred interviews with decision makers, is not a list of what you should do, it is a list of what they are looking for. If you're in the right place, at the right time, doing the right things, they will see those qualities in you. Why? Simply, because those are the qualities that they're looking for.

A hiring manager will see the qualities that they are looking for

The requirements of your role are a given, they are the baseline that you must achieve. You are unlikely to achieve significant career advancement by simply doing your job, because that's what you're paid to do.

High potentials achieve more than this. In particular, a high potential will seek greater responsibility from both their direct line manager and their indirect managers, and that greater responsibility creates opportunities to show capabilities which go beyond the basic job description. A high potential will not simply do more of their current job; that would be counter-productive.

Trying to emulate a long list of behaviours will be fruitless because you don't have the missing piece of the puzzle – the actions that the leader associates with those qualities. Being a good communicator seems obvious, yet you will likely find that what you think of as good communication is very different to what a decision maker thinks, and it's what they think that is important. If you're talking to a decision maker and mapping out their decision making preferences, you can at least ask them to give you specific examples, however if you don't have direct access then it's better not to guess, because you'll certainly be wrong.

Let's look at the list of high potential qualities in more detail, and see what information we can glean from them which might be helpful for you.

Attention to detail

Detail is always relative to a surrounding frame of reference, so attending to detail is not, in itself, a behaviour that you can emulate without knowing what the frame of reference is. You can easily focus on too small a level of detail. We might therefore interpret this quality as a way of saying that you don't make mistakes by missing important facts, and the importance of not making mistakes is that you don't provide information to your boss which causes him or her embarrassment. Your focus should therefore be on double checking facts which have a bearing on your manager's credibility.

Team player, collaborative, build relationships

A manager wants his or her team to get along. Friction and conflict are time consuming, distracting, and ultimately pointless. Being easy to work with might cause you frustration from time to time, but it's much less effort for you in the long run. The risk you face is in getting lost in the team and having your efforts go unnoticed. Political players will often manipulate conflict so that they can be seen as the voice of reason, the person who brings harmony back to the team.

Accountability, integrity

Ultimately, doing what you say you're going to do builds trust. If you do not hold yourself accountable for your actions then you can never learn from your mistakes. Blaming others is definitely a career-limiting behaviour. A consequence of accountability is that you communicate quickly and clearly if you are unable to do what you have promised. There is no such thing as "beyond your control" because you control either the action leading to the result, or you control your communication. Failure is never a surprise for the high potential – or their manager.

Alignment, customer focus

Many people say that they are customer focused, when it's more likely that they are KPI focused, and those KPIs relate to a customer metric such as a sales revenue or service quality. In reality, being entirely customer focused is not a good idea for any business because you can't focus on every customer and the result is often that the customers who shout loudest get the most attention while no-one notices the quieter customers going to your competitors. Instead of focusing on the customer directly, focus on the actions which create strong capabilities in the business, which is ultimately what your customers want and has the advantageous side effect of building a legacy that you can talk about in your next job interview. Don't just fix the problem, build a system that fixes the problem.

Open minded, approachable, good listener

If your mind was open, you would never make a decision. Therefore, the decision maker doesn't want your mind to be open to everyone, they only want your mind to be open to them. Take their advice and say thank you.

Business knowledge

A good all-round knowledge of your business is vital, especially if you work in a support function such as IT, finance or HR. It's sadly quite common for support staff to have no idea what their employer does. You can develop your business knowledge very easily by asking for secondment and buddying opportunities, and simply by talking to the people around you about their jobs. Your genuine curiosity will be rewarded with open access to valuable career information.

Strength, persistence, flexibility

Strength and flexibility go hand in hand because you need the strength to push past obstacles whilst also having the flexibility to work around hard blocks. The problem is that blind persistence can lead to people continuing to pursue a pointless course of action, and too much flexibility can lead to excessive changes in direction, which can appear as indecisiveness. The ideal compromise can be found in your relentless focus on the end goal, the ultimate objective, and flexibility in how you achieve that. Remember that bending the corporate rules is good when you're winning and making your boss look good, but don't bend them so far that you make yourself a scapegoat for any future fallout.

Delegate, develop your team

The fundamental role of a manager is to delegate, and this is reflected in organisational hierarchies. In modern organisations, managers also have their own operational responsibilities too, which can lead to conflicts of interest. Delegating is probably the most important development activity for a team, and it's also the activity that most managers get wrong. Most managers delegate tasks which leads to micro-management. Instead, focus on delegating authority which frees up your own time and provides your team with space to learn and grow.

A simple way to remember how to delegate effectively is to give your team AIR:

A I R

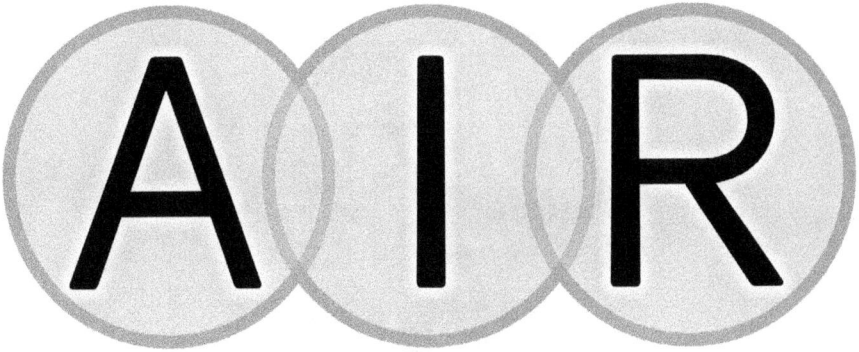

Authority   Information   Result

To delegate effectively, give the Authority and the Information necessary in order to achieve the end Result.

Micro-managers don't give Authority or Information, they give precise instructions. This isn't delegating, it's treating your team as if they're robots. The greatest value of having people in an organisation is that they are innovators and problem solvers. Your team multiplies your capability. If you ever think, "It would be quicker to do it myself than to explain it" then you have missed the point about delegating.

Delegation is your most important tool for developing the capabilities of your team. A popular development approach, called the 70:20:10 model, tells us that 70% of development opportunities arise from on-the-job learning, through problem solving and facing new challenges. 20% of development can come from peer learning activities such as mentoring, and only 10% comes from classroom training activities.

10% Formal training

Peer learning Mentoring 20%

Workplace experience 70%

You can turn any activity into a learning opportunity with a simple question that gets the learner to reflect on their experience:

"What did you learn?"

Later on in this book, we will discuss how you can make the most of planned learning activities such as training and mentoring, where you will learn why this is such an important and valuable question.

Decisive, analytical

One of the aspects of business which has changed radically since the widespread adoption of computers in the 1990s is the sheer volume of information available to managers. Whilst this seems to support better decisions, the overwhelming nature of so much information often has the opposite effect. If managers cannot make sense of information, they will rely on personal judgements, which are loaded with bias and prejudice. The more raw data you are presented with, the easier it is for you to find exactly the information you're looking for in order to support the biased decisions that you have already made.

One of the most important things that a manager can do is to create objective decision making systems which aim to remove bias. Bias is always present in some form because these systems are created by humans, and humans are biased. Amazon famously had to take their recruitment AI offline after realising that it was racist, because the thousands of previous hiring decisions that it analysed in order to learn its decision rules were similarly biased – not because Amazon has racist recruiters, but because Amazon has human recruiters and humans are naturally drawn to similarity.

The qualities of 'decisive' and 'analytical' might seem to be incompatible. Analysis takes time, but managers are often under pressure to act quickly, and get it right. This apparent incompatibility is easily resolved when we realise that you have never made a 'right' decision in your whole life. You have made decisions. Afterwards, you took the actions necessary to turn those decisions into results. In short, you will never make the right decision, you will only make a decision, and then you will do what it takes to make it right.

Indecision, or changing a decision after is has been made, introduces delay, it creates doubt and mistrust and these get in the way of the clear action needed to make a decision work. If your decisions don't lead to the results you were expecting, it's not because your decisions were wrong, it's because you lacked the commitment to make your decisions work. Mentors can be of great support to you in this, by sharing the mistakes they made – mistakes which you will surely repeat if you don't learn from them.

In short, use the experience of mentors to make decision making systems, use those systems consistently and take the actions necessary to make your decisions work out as you planned.

Passionate

Passion doesn't mean energy, it means suffering. How do you know that someone has passion for their work? Is it because they bounce into the office every morning, full of energy and drive? That's simply not sustainable. We observe passion when we see someone dedicating themselves to their interests, enduring the ups and downs of life. We see them persevering when the going gets tough. We see them committing themselves to their cause. Passion isn't a feeling, it's a judgement that the observer places on you. When the decision maker sees you sticking with it when things get rough, when they see you carrying on when others give up, they call that passion. Therefore, from your point of view, passion is more accurately described as resilience.

Superficially, it is easy to confuse passion with enthusiasm, however one observation that we have made from many tens of thousands of coaching hours is that the more enthusiastic a person seems about a task, the less likely they are to complete it. A politically motivated, insecure leader will be delighted when a member of their team picks up their latest crazy idea with gusto. It doesn't matter that no action is taken, it's the enthusiastic support, the person endorsement which matters. A leader like this will not support your career growth – they are far too busy worrying about their own. A leader who surrounds themselves with 'yes men', a team who endorse whatever the leader says, has a vested interest in keeping that team exactly where they are. As far as your career and your survival are concerned, a leader who rewards results is far more useful than a leader who rewards loyalty. Just be sure to deliver!

The paradox with passion is that you also have to know when you are chasing a lost cause. Passion at the expense of results won't get you very far. How do you know when to persist and when to call it a day? First, ask your mentor. Second, ask yourself why you started on this journey. For example, if you pick up a project which other people have given up on, do you clearly understand why it's important to you, and what you think you're going to get out of it? As soon as you lose sight of that, your passion has clouded your judgement.

Focus on goals, KPIs

High performers in any role, in any industry, in any country are not the people who work hardest, or are the smartest, or are the best educated. The highest performers are the people whose behaviour aligns with what the organisation measures.

Unfortunately, what the organisation says it measures isn't always what it regards as important. There are both explicit measures, such as sales targets, and tacit measures, such as time spent in the office.

It's therefore entirely possible that you could achieve your explicit KPIs and still not see career progress, whereas your colleagues who focus on the tacit KPIs are rewarded with new opportunities. You might feel frustrated about this, even resentful, because this is clearly unfair.

If you ask any business leader where sales targets come from, they might tell you that the organisation's costs and profit targets are analysed and divided amongst sales territories. If this were true then a sales target would be a number such as $237,193.89 however you're more likely to see a target of $250,000. What does this tell you? Essentially, if a target is expressed as a round number, it's fabricated, made up to incentivise you. If you miss a target, can you expect to be fired? The amount of leeway that exists around your explicit targets depends on how effective you are at delivering on your tacit targets.

When business is good, no-one's job is under threat. When times are tough and a manager is told to lose staff, who will she or he prioritise? Logically, a manager will retain the staff who are the highest performers. In practice, the manager may retain the staff who are most likely to protect the manager. Therefore, it would be wise to allocate at least some of your time and focus to determining your manager's tacit KPIs and measures so that you can prioritise the critical deliverables for your role.

Fast to decide and act

When there's a crisis such as a major customer breakdown, many managers will favour action over analysis. Of course, this then creates another problem, that the fast action was the wrong action. Humans are evolved with the skill of mental rehearsal, and the way that we act quickly in dangerous situations is by acting out decisions that we have already made.

The effective leader therefore solves the paradox of acting quickly yet analytically through regular scenario planning. Rather than by hoping for the best, the effective leader will consider the worst case scenarios and prepare action plans in advance. At a time of crisis, the leader appears to act decisively, when in reality she or he is simply applying a decision framework that they had already created, outside of a time of pressure.

This is exactly what happens in every office when a fire drill is conducted. We don't want to wait until there's an emergency to figure out how to get out of the building so we get people to rehearse at a time of safety. If a fire breaks out, people will of course still panic and get confused, but there is more of a chance that some people will remember the drills, read the signs, act rationally and that others will follow them to safety.

Creative

Another common paradox in business is the conflict between consistency and innovation. Managers often want their staff to show initiative, but only if that initiative leads to the right results. In other cases, the manager might say, "Why didn't you stick to what works?" and this can be extremely frustrating, especially if your manager has a very distant, 'hands off' approach except for when things go wrong. The key to managing this paradox effectively is communication. All too often, a combination of organisational culture and personal upbringing can cause a person to keep their plans to themselves, thinking that if the plan doesn't work out then no-one will be any the wiser, and if the plan does work out then they can then expect praise. However, this is often not the case. It's just as likely that you will get the blame for failure whilst someone else takes the credit for your innovation. Ultimately, what most leaders want is to be kept informed, because information builds trust.

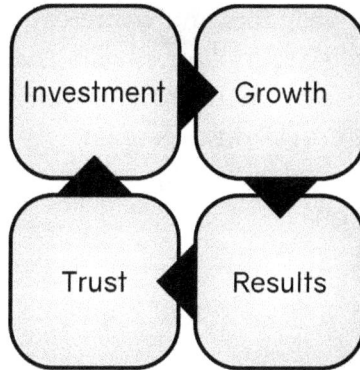

If you keep your manager in the loop, you will guard against the most difficult situation of all – leaving your manager exposed when her or his manager asks what's going on with a particular project or customer. By building trust, you are encouraging your manager to give you more space for your creativity, which is an investment in you. When that investment pays off, you share the credit with your manager. If your new idea fails, your manager is more likely to frame it as a valuable learning experience because you have not exposed them to risk without their knowledge.

In reality, there are very few new ideas in business. Every new product or concept builds upon elements that came before. The iPhone seemed revolutionary back in 2007 but it was simply a repackaging of other components which had long been in use in other products. The Psion Organiser, the PalmPilot, the Compaq iPaq all predated the iPhone by many years, however network and battery technologies limited their utility. The perfect storm of network availability, battery life, hardware and user demand created the success of the iPhone, not the engineers at Apple. The creative leader therefore immerses themselves in the world of innovation, rather than limiting themselves to the press releases of their own employer. Whatever industry you work in, subscribe to newsletters from a variety of other industries. Get to know what's happening around the world. Follow thought leaders through their blogs and podcasts. Get into the habit of thinking that if something new is happening in finance, for example, then before long it will also impact on pharmaceuticals and agriculture. Join webinars and conferences, and consider the impact that emerging technologies will have within your own business. It's really not difficult to "stay ahead of the curve" if you simply keep your eyes and ears open.

Good communication

Being a good communicator has very little to do with being loud, clear, impactful or sincere. Good communication is fast, honest and empathic. Above all else, you have to remember that being a good communicator means that you focus not on what you want to say but on what the other person needs to hear. From your manager's point of view, it's likely that good communication means that you share all of your secrets with them but with no-one else. If you know something that will affect their reputation, you are expected to tell them right away, but with tact. As a general rule, managers don't like surprises. Communication is of course a two-way process, so being a good listener must be part of good communication, and listening to your boss will create many surprising opportunities for you. When you simply listen, it's really quite amazing what people will tell you.

Time management, multitasking

What do you think of when you imagine someone who is good at time management? Perhaps someone who is extremely busy yet not stressed? They are balancing their priorities. In other words, no matter how busy they are, they never say no to their boss.

The challenge from your point of view is that you fully understand the importance of doing everything your boss asks you to do, but you also appreciate having a life outside of work. The more you do, the more people expect you to do. The busier you allow yourself to be, the more work people will give you. We know manager senior managers who have suffered serious health problems as a direct result of their inability to say no. Clearly there has to be a compromise.

Here is a very simple trick that you can always use when balancing your priorities. The essence of the approach is to understand that time is a limited, valuable commodity and can not be given or taken. You will always have the same amount of time, regardless of what you do with it. Therefore, you are not managing time but priorities. When a manager wants you to be better at time management, they often mean that they want you to prioritise the things that they think are important. We've already mentioned one organisation where people were rewarded for saying yes, regardless of whether they delivered on their promises or not.

Once we treat time as a commodity, we realise that it can be traded, it becomes negotiable. Now, instead of being stuck in an uncomfortable dilemma, you can create more choice. Instead of being limited to saying "yes" or "no", you can use the magic word that is used in every successful negotiation; "if".

Personal learning

Arrogance literally means 'not questioning', and it's the opposite to an openness to learning. We mention this because we find that these two traits are mutually exclusive. The person who defends their own knowledge and tries to prove that they 'know it all' does not ask questions or show curiosity. This reveals a stagnant mindset, and an unwillingness to embrace change. The leader's desire for the trait of personal learning could be a response to the need to keep up in an ever-changing working culture, or it could be a response to the leader's desire to share their own hard-won lessons with their successor. Either way, it's a valuable behaviour to develop.

Cultural adaptation

We can define culture as the language and rules of a particular environment, which could be an organisation or a locality. Being able to navigate cultural differences is an incredibly valuable skill, especially when working with multinational organisations, or when dealing with mergers and acquisitions.

In today's increasingly globalised business environment, almost all organisations are multinational, and almost all are in some way affected by organisational mergers and acquisitions. Therefore, developing your cultural awareness and flexibility is a vital career skill, regardless of where in the world you work.

Healthy

One decision maker thought that it was important for high potential candidates to look after their bodies and keep fit. This is a good example of the decision maker projecting their own values onto their chosen candidates. Keeping fit may or may not be important to you, and that may or may not have anything to do with your leadership potential. Perhaps that one leader thought that if you take care of your body then you must have discipline, self respect and physical stamina. Perhaps, for them, health is a short cut to other qualities. Perhaps the gym or the squash court are good venues to develop political connections. Whatever the reason, you can see the importance of asking, rather than simply chasing a superficial quality which may or may not align with your own personal aspirations.

Mentoring and Development

One of the most valuable steps that you can take in accelerating your career development is to work with a mentor.

Let's define a mentor as, "Someone who supports you in your personal or career development who is not your line manager."

A mentoring relationship could be either formal or informal:

- Formal – planned, scheduled and recorded conversations which form part of a long term development plan

- Informal – chance, unscheduled conversations which help you to clarify an issue or resolve a short term problem

While a mentor is an important role, it is not the only role which plays a part in a person's development.

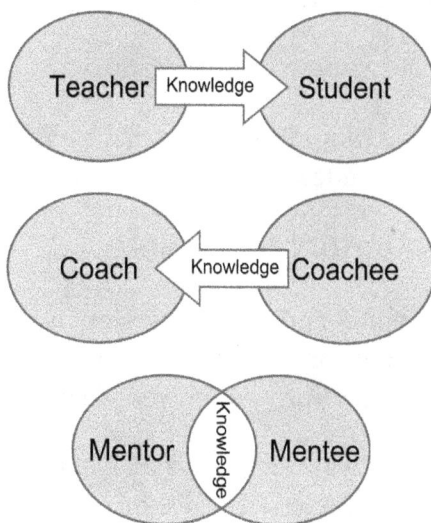

The role of a mentor is therefore not one that we define through the mentor's behaviour but through the **relationship** that they form with a mentee.

The mentor does not have a direct vested interest in your success. They will ensure that you maintain accountability for your actions and your outcomes, and they will utilise their life experience to support your self-driven learning.

Guidelines for mentoring

Here are some points to help you to make the most of the opportunity for mentoring.

- Your development is your responsibility

- A mentor can't tell you what to do, that would mean you're not responsible for the result

- A mentor does not judge you

- If you aren't honest about where you are then the mentor can't help you move forwards

- If you aren't honest about your goals then the mentor can't help you achieve them

- Feedback is a source of information to help you navigate

- Success is a temporary illusion, failure is the best outcome because you will learn the most from it

Matching the mentor and mentee

Mentors have strengths and weaknesses as much as anyone, and you should not focus on finding the 'perfect' mentor but on finding the right mentor for your current needs.

The following model was developed by Michael Heath based on research that he conducted for his book *The Fit Mentor*. The model is based on two characteristic needs of a mentee:

Task Expertise is the knowledge that a mentor may have that is related to the occupational activities of a mentee.

Facilitative Expertise is the mentor's ability to engage with the mentee using a variety of interpersonal techniques that stimulate reflection and opportunities for growth.

The following diagram illustrates the four mentoring Styles which are explored in more detail on the following pages.

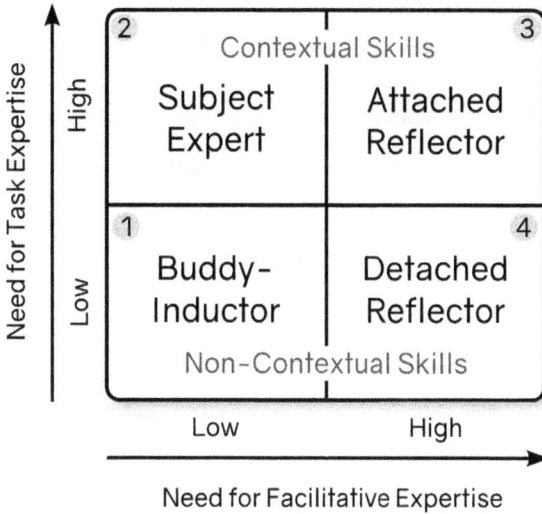

	Contextual Skills	
2 Subject Expert		**3** Attached Reflector
1 Buddy-Inductor		**4** Detached Reflector
	Non-Contextual Skills	

Need for Task Expertise (High / Low)

Low — High

Need for Facilitative Expertise

Four mentoring styles

Mentoring Style 1: Buddy-Inductor

This mentor acts as a supporter and guide for new members of staff, helping them settle in to a new role.

The original source of the term 'Mentor' is the friend of Odysseus' who looked after Odysseus' son, so the 'adult-child' relationship is closer to buddying than the 'adult-to-adult' relationship that we now associate with the term 'Mentoring'.

Likely Mentor Background

The Buddy-Inductor is usually assigned to make someone, typically a new hire, feel welcome to an organisation or team. They are likely to have little or no authority over the mentee.

Value of the Relationship to the Mentee

- Learn the job faster
- Remain enthusiastic and motivated
- Contribute new perspectives earlier

Value of the Relationship to the Mentor

- Feel valued for their experience

- Share knowledge and experiences

- Build relationships

Value of the Relationship to the Organisation

- Individuals integrate into the organisation and reach a level of autonomy earlier

- Fresh perspectives provide valuable insights to organisations

Probable Relationship

- Colleague

Main Mentoring Activities

- Informs

- Warns

- Advises

- Guides

Mentee's need from the relationship

- Low task, Low reflective

Mentoring Style 2: Subject Expert

Often, the mentee will avoid any conversation around personal development and only seeks to have their technical questions answered. A Subject Expert mentor could be a line manager or perhaps a peer with superior expertise in a given area.

Likely Mentor Background

The mentor is likely to be a more experienced colleague or perhaps a past colleague who still works in the same field. The mentee will usually seek their help rather than the mentor having responsibility for 'driving' the relationship.

Value of the Relationship to the Mentee

- Gains skills or knowledge specific to role

- Develops quicker with support in specific subject areas

Value of the Relationship to the Mentor
- Feel valued for their knowledge
- Gains insights from a fresh perspective
- Able to practise the skills required in this area, e.g. providing constructive feedback

Value of the Relationship to the Organisation
- Individuals integrate into the organisation and reach a level of autonomy earlier
- Knowledge, experience and skills are shared

Probable Relationship
- Manager or colleague

Main Mentoring Activities
- Teaches
- Instructs
- Trains
- Gives feedback

Mentee's need from the relationship
- High task, Low reflective

Mentoring Style 3: Attached Reflector

An Attached Reflector is more consistent with how managers often view a Mentor. They are often closely related in the hierarchy, perhaps a manager's manager or peer, and possess a considerable level of knowledge about the mentee's work. They differ from the Subject Expert in that they are only generally aware of the day-to-day work of their mentee, but can bring complementary experience to any issue. Their role is not to tell, but to ask the right questions and stimulate intellectual development from the mentee.

Likely Mentor Background

An authority on the mentee's area of expertise, they are often valued as 'sounding boards' for the mentee's ideas and aspirations about their work. Being separated from direct managerial responsibility for the mentee, they see their role as one of a 'knowledgeable authority' to help them think more widely about what they do and how it fits into the 'bigger picture'.

Value of the Relationship to the Mentee

- Gains a breadth and depth of thinking
- Contextualises and shapes ideas and gains guidance in approach

Value of the Relationship to the Mentor

- Provides an opportunity for practising skills e.g. coaching.
- Contributes to an individual's growth
- Gains insights into their own thinking

Value of the Relationship to the Organisation

- Encourages strong internal relationships and reflective practice

Probable Relationship

- Departmental Director

Main Mentoring Activities

- Coaches
- Listens
- Advises
- Guides
- Feeds back

Mentee's need from the relationship

- High task, High reflective

Mentoring Style 4: Detached Reflector

The Detached Reflector stimulates reflection and encourages the mental processes of the mentee, but they differ in one key aspect; they have little or no knowledge of the mentee's work, and this is their strength.

Sometimes, a mentor can be too close to a subject to be able to take 'the long view' of it. A Detached Reflector has no agenda to pursue as they are not part of the general politics of the organisation. Such a distance has many advantages for the mentee, particularly in offering the mentee confidentiality.

It is more likely that this type of mentor is sought independently by the mentee and consequently will be valued more highly.

Likely Mentor Background

Respected for their thinking and the ability to deepen the thinking of others. They have no contact with any aspect of the mentee's work, yet are valued for their ability to help the mentee reflect on issues in the broadest possible sense. Being detached from the mentee's workplace, they can let the mentee look deeply at all aspects of their work with complete confidentiality.

Value of the Relationship to the Mentee

• Gains an objective view in absolute confidence

Value of the Relationship to the Mentor

• Gains an objective view without bias in absolute confidence

Value of the Relationship to the Organisation

• Encourages individuals to network and build relationships that encourage a breadth of organisational thinking

Probable Relationship

• Senior or respected figure from an unrelated part of the business

Main Mentoring Activities

• Coaches

• Listens

• Advises

• Guides

• Offers feedback

Mentee's need from the relationship

• Low task, High reflective

Mentee-Mentor mismatches

It is important to match the mentee with the mentor they *need*, not necessarily the mentor they *want*.

Perhaps every leadership candidate wants to be mentored by the CEO, but this isn't feasible, and the CEO does not necessarily have good facilitation skills. A peer may even be a better mentor, so we have to overcome the mentee's expectation that having a mentor is a sign of status, and therefore they should have the most 'important' mentor available.

A mismatch can be caused by many factors:

- The mentee chooses a mentor based on liking rather than developmental value

- The manager chooses a mentor without consulting or considering the needs of the mentee

- The needs of the mentee were not properly explored at the outset

- The manager chooses someone with whom they enjoyed a close relationship in order to maintain control of the situation

- A mentor is assigned who knows the mentee personally, perhaps from a previous role

A very common issue in mentoring is where organisations create a formal mentoring program and allocate mentors to high potentials. Once the candidates for the program have been told that they are high potentials, they lose their incentive for making any personal development effort - they have already 'made it'. What they then seek from a mentor is merely introductions that will speed them on their career journey. The mentor becomes frustrated that the mentee doesn't listen or act on feedback, the mentee becomes frustrated that their mentor isn't opening enough doors for them and the program fails with the conclusion that 'mentoring doesn't work'. In this example, you can easily see that the failure is not because of the concept of mentoring but because of the mismatch of expectations, partly caused by setting unrealistic expectations.

Consider a scenario; you have been nominated for a career development program. The program is described as an intensive, remedial personal training system that will correct your shortcomings and better prepare you for progression within your organisation. How appealing does this sound to you?

Consider a second scenario; you have been nominated for a career development program. The program is described as an intensive, aspirational personal training system that will build on your strengths and create a success pathway for you within your organisation. How appealing does this sound to you?

If you were offered a place on either program, which would you choose, and why?

You already know that it's a trick question; they are descriptions of the same program. All that has changed is the benchmark to which you are being compared.

Accepting and asking for feedback

One of the biggest challenges that a mentor faces is getting their mentee to accept feedback. We all have a self image, and we feel very uncomfortable and defensive when that self image is challenged. Similarly, one of your biggest challenges in working with a mentor is in overcoming your own cognitive biases and accepting their feedback. It helps to understand that their feedback is neither objectively true nor false, however it is useful. Despite your carefully crafted self-image, you have never seen yourself, and you really don't know how you appear to others. Since you depend on others to recognise, hire and promote you, their opinion of you really is important.

Sometimes, you might have to teach your mentor to give you better feedback; feedback that is more objective than subjective.

Subjective = Relative to your own perceptions, views, values, beliefs and judgements:

"Your presentation was too short"

"You were too nervous"

Objective = Defined by external standards and criteria:

"Your presentation lasted for 93 seconds"

"You repeated the subject of your presentation three times"

A simple test is this: if you can add the words "for me" to the end of the feedback, it's subjective:

"Your presentation lasted for 93 seconds for me" = Objective, because "for me" makes no sense

"Your presentation was too short for me" = Subjective, because "for me" makes sense

Unsolicited feedback will almost always be subjective because the person offering you the feedback is emotional responding to their own perceptions and judgements. You can easily convert any feedback into a more objective or useful format with a simple question.

Firstly, it is very important to acknowledge the feedback rather than rejecting it, regardless of how it might make you feel. If you reject feedback, you will teach the person to stop giving you feedback and you will cut yourself off from a valuable source of external data.

Consider what it's like when you give a friend well intentioned advice and they keep rejecting it by saying, "Yeah, yeah, I know" or "You don't understand". After a short time, you feel frustrated and you stop offering advice. You might even say to yourself, "Well, it's their problem, they'll have to find out the hard way".

Therefore, it's important to encourage people to offer you feedback as much as possible if you are to accelerate your development, and since people will generally do more of what you give them recognition for, the simplest way to encourage more feedback is to acknowledge it.

Secondly, the most useful feedback is actionable. If someone tells you that you have done something wrong then they are of course comparing you to some standard or expectation. Knowing that your action was wrong is not helpful unless you also have visibility of that standard and know what you could or should have done instead. Therefore, you will also benefit from converting the feedback into a more positive, actionable format.

Thirdly, subjective feedback is relative to the reality of the person giving you the feedback. The relevance of the information is obvious to them but it might not be obvious to you. In this case, you might need them to be more specific about the meaning and relevance of the feedback being offered. This does of course give you a valuable insight into their reality, particularly their life experiences through which they have learned the standards and expectations which they are now projecting onto you.

The format of your question is therefore:

Acknowledge → Reformat

For example:

Feedback: You're not engaged enough

Question: Thank you! What do you suggest I do differently?

Feedback: You're not talking to the right people

Question: Thank you! How is that information useful for me?

Judgement and bias

Bias is part of any relationship. We all have preferences, and we all have knowledge and experiences which influence how we see the world and the people around us.

Whilst everyone is biased, for a mentor this is dangerous and it is one of the important reasons why a mentor must never fall into the trap of giving the mentee easy answers, as in telling the mentee what to do. What worked in the past, in a different situation for the mentor is not what will work for the mentee. Similarly, when you are seeking a mentor, you would be wise to avoid questions such as "What should I do?".

For mentoring to be effective, both the mentor and the mentee must bring their experiences together to create something new.

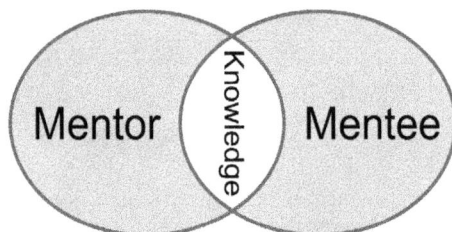

In mentoring and coaching, there is no right and wrong, no true or false. For people in a technical role, this can be difficult to put into practice because a red wire always means something specific, and a mathematical formula always gives the correct answer. When we're dealing with technical facts, we can debate who is right and wrong. However, as soon as we involve people in those equations, we introduce subjective perspectives, individual experiences and of course opinions based not on fact but on feelings. Once we scale up any technical design, the more complex it becomes, the more subjective the design decisions become. You only need to take a look at the conversations in technical discussion forums to see that there really are no simple answers.

We cannot remove bias, because we are, in our nature, subjective observers of the world. What we can do is to welcome, acknowledge and accept our bias, and use it to work with us rather than against us.

A mentor's role is to support you, and to do that they must see you as you *really* are, not as you *want* to be seen. Only then can you get the support you need in becoming all that you *can* be.

Creating activities that challenge

Even regular mentoring sessions represent a tiny proportion of your working time:

Frequency	Percentage of working time	
One hour per week	2.5%	
One hour per month	0.6%	

Therefore, you will realistically achieve very little progress if you believe that you have to complete everything within the mentoring session itself.

Instead, if you think about the mentoring session as a time to review past actions and agree future actions which you believe will aid in your development, then we have much more time available. Every moment of every working day can be an opportunity to learn and practice something new that will support your development.

You will therefore need to create challenging actions and activities which drive learning and growth and this is an area where your mentor can perhaps offer you the most value. Your mentor can potentially see new challenges which you are, as yet, unaware of. Asking for assignments is therefore an excellent way to focus the mentoring relationship on action.

The mentor-manager partnership

Your line manager has a vested interest in your success. If you excel in your job then your KPIs and objectives are aligned with those of your manager and you both win. If you excel to the extent that you are promoted then your manager is seen as someone who develops their team, making your vacated role more desirable for the next candidate and bringing fresh ideas into the team.

A good mentoring relationship actually involves three people, working together; the mentee, the mentor, and the mentee's line manager. Even if you seek out a mentor by yourself, it's a good idea to involve your line manager in the initial conversation, or at the very least to let them know what you're doing. At the very least, you are signalling that you are serious about your career development and that you are taking a leading role in your future success, rather than waiting for your manager to send you on another training course.

Ultimately, your line manager is the arbiter of your success. They create the environment within which you operate and they judge your performance against your KPIs. You don't have to like them in order to do a good job, and they don't have to like you in order to treat you with respect.

Some managers might welcome a close relationship with the mentor, other managers might only want occasional feedback. Keeping your manager involved on any level is a very good idea. In fact, why not involve all of your career stakeholders?

In mentoring, you may choose to share thoughts which you feel you cannot share with your manager. The mentor must therefore always work with discretion and treat the mentoring sessions as confidential, otherwise you will quickly feel that you cannot trust anyone and your career progress will stagnate.

You can agree ground rules at the beginning of the relationship. Should the mentor give feedback to the manager if asked? What

Mentoring and Development

should the boundaries be? Should this always take place within a three way conversation so that you know what is being said about you? If everyone is truly open, and committed to success then why would this be a problem?

Neither the manager nor the mentor are responsible for your development. Only you are responsible for your development, and the manager and mentor's responsibility is to work together effectively to give you every opportunity for success.

Development opportunities

If you are actively seeking career development then it is almost inevitable that you will find yourself nominated for development opportunities such as talent, training or coaching programs. It's therefore wise to consider how you can make the best use of such opportunities, both in terms of the program content and in terms of how you visibly engage with them.

The authors of this book have more than 40 years combined experience in developing and delivering such programs, and probably more like 70 years experience as students and consumers. We're going to share some 'insider secrets' with you which will definitely help you to get more from such programs.

We'll organise our advice into a series of tips.

You are not being assessed

Your manager, or HR rep, or the program provider themselves will tell you that the training or coaching is not an assessment, it is merely an opportunity for you to consume developmental content. This is a lie. You are being assessed.

Here's a message that we received just days ago from a manager who had placed some of their team members onto a development program. "Can you tell me more later about them once you interact with them - personality, way of working, strength/ weakness etc."

You might say that this is an example of a good manager-mentor relationship, where the manager is seeking feedback from an independent source. You might also say that the trainer's feedback will play a part in the career opportunities made available to those students. A good trainer will attempt to be objective, impartial and kind, to build on the students' strengths and offer options and possible consequences. A less tactful or politically aware trainer might see an opportunity to please and impress their client with a series of insightful character assassinations. Therefore, as the student, you are in a difficult situation. You have to assume that the trainer or coach will report back to your manager, within the limitations of any confidentiality agreements, and you have to assume that they will be smart enough to see through any pretence or performance that you put on to impress them.

In short, pay attention and just be yourself, which is good advice if you are a smart, professional student who is willing to open up to new learning. If you're an idiot then 'be yourself' is probably not good advice. You're not an idiot though, are you? It's a trick question - remember Dunning-Kruger. If you are an idiot then you don't know it and if you admit to being an idiot then you're not an idiot. You can't win.

The key is to understand the criteria that you are being assessed against, and for that we must step into the shoes of the trainer or coach. They have been hired to do a job and their success depends on them doing that job effectively. To achieve that, they need you to play your part. They need you to turn up on time, pay attention, ask questions that show you're thinking about how to apply what you're learning and be kind to other program participants.

Meanwhile, you have made an assumption about why you have been selected for the program, and you will act based on that assumption. For example, if you think that the program is remedial, you will avoid attending, you will show off your superior knowledge and you will fail to complete any tasks or assignments. Any behaviour which aims to prove that you don't need to be there, you already know it all and your job is far too important to waste time in training will backfire on you. The simplest thing that you can do is to consciously make an assumption which serves your greater purpose of career progression, such as "I have been selected for this program because I am open to learning, I am a good role model for my colleagues and I will never know what I don't know". Adopting this as a working assumption is more likely to result in a positive assessment.

Think back to your past experiences of training programs. Do you remember the know-all who would pompously answer every question? Do you remember the person who kept leaving the room to make urgent calls to show how important their job was? Do you remember the person who made jokes and distracted others to hide the fact that they felt out of their depth? Do you remember the person who asked pointless, diverting questions in order to delay or derail the training? That person was you, from the point of view of the other students.

Let's review some of the top characteristics that leaders are looking for in their high potentials; Effective communication, Ownership, Acceptance within team, Team work, Positive approach. As a minimum, these are the standards that you are being assessed against.

You do not know it already

As previously mentioned, many students attending corporate training programs will assume that their attendance is the result of a deficiency on their part. Firstly, this may not be the case where there is an identified development need within a team. Secondly, this probably is the case, and you might appreciate that when you stop being defensive. Whatever the subject of the training, you are not an expert. The purpose of most training is not to make you an expert. Most training falls into one of two categories in terms of its true purpose; compliance or culture.

Compliance is easy to understand. Your employer's insurance broker requires every company car driver to attend a safe driving course, so you're 'sent' on that course, whether you are a 'good' driver or not. Your employer's industry regulator requires every employee who interacts with client data to attend data protection training. You attend the training, the compliance manager ticks a box, everyone is happy. This is the type of training that seems most likely to attract what trainers call 'hostages', people who are there but say that they don't want to be there, people who would rather be at their desks doing their jobs. This is an illusion. When compliance affects your job, training *is* your job. It is not time wasted. It is time invested in your professional reputation.

Culture is a very different type of training. Typically, you will see less PowerPoint and more group activities, less pop quizzes and more assignments. If you've ever attended leadership or management development programs, strategic sales training, presentation skills, time management or anything loosely termed 'soft skills' training then you have experienced culture training. A minority of corporate trainers are skilled enough to effectively facilitate this type of training, so if you attended training in the early part of your career then it was probably run in the style of compliance training, giving you off-the-shelf ways of working and simple checklists for success. You probably found such training less than useful.

This second category relates to culture because changing the way that managers manage or the way that sales people sell creates a change in the collective behaviour of a team or organisation, and this is one of the ways in which we define an organisational culture. If we teach managers to give constructive feedback instead of criticising mistakes then we have changed the dynamics of management relationships., which changes the operating rules within the organisation, which is a change in culture. Some organisational leaders naively think that they can procure management training to make people more efficient managers without changing the culture, however this is only possible if the program is carefully designed to align with the rules of the current culture.

For the student who resents being sent on a training course because they think that their current level of knowledge is not being appreciated, this raises two possibilities. Either the training is of the compliance type, in which case it doesn't matter what you already know, or it is of the culture type, in which case it doesn't matter what you already know.

In short, you are not being 'sent' on a corporate training course because you don't know enough, therefore you are wasting your time trying to show anyone what you already know. Relax, enjoy the different perspectives and take the opportunity to show what a committed, diligent and thoughtful learner you are.

You haven't made it

You have been selected for a development program because of your potential. You still have to prove that you can live up to that potential. You have most likely been nominated as a high potential because of the results and attitude that you have demonstrated so far, however the actions that got you here are not necessarily the actions that will get you to the next level.

Being nominated as a high potential is not a reward.

It is a challenge, a call to adventure.

The learning cycle

In 1984, David Kolb and Ron Fry published Kolb's Experiential Learning Model (ELM). Kolb's work is greatly respected across many learning fields, from schools to professional education and therefore forms the basis of much of the structured learning that you will experience in your career. The ELM presents a four part learning cycle.

Concrete Experience - Feel

This stage is one of real, physical, direct, first hand, visceral sensory experience. An experience might comprise any combination of sights, sounds, feelings, tastes or smells and in fact, you may know that all experiences and therefore all memories comprise all of these elements, even though some of them may be less prominent than others. A concrete experience is external to us and therefore always in the present.

Reflective Observation - Watch

Once we've had a concrete experience, we reflect on it. We cast our mind back, both consciously and unconsciously, and relive the experience so that we can make generalisations and draw conclusions. Research has shown that the structure within the brain known as the hippocampus creates a kind of 'action replay' of emotionally charged events, etching them forever in our long term memories. Reflective observation is internal and therefore in the past, and the observation isn't necessarily visual, it features all of the sensory information which was originally present.

Abstract Concept - Think

Having relived the experience, we take those generalisations and conclusions and use them to create an abstract concept, a set of rules or principles which govern the experience and others like it. When abstract conceptualisation involves mental rehearsal, it is internal and appears to be in the future, when in fact it is a replay of the past as the future doesn't yet exist.

Active Experiment - Do

We take the abstract concept and test it by applying it to new situations. A child tests a range of household objects to find out if they float as well as his lost balloon. A father gives all of the house plants a close shave in order to 'try out' the new hedge trimmer that he received for his birthday. Active experimentation leads full circle to a new concrete experience which either affirms or contradicts the abstract concept. Active experimentation is always external and in the present.

We could perhaps say that the sequence of events is:

1. Do something

2. Get feedback

3. Review feedback

4. Make a plan

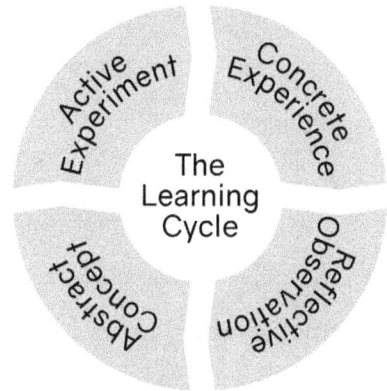

The Learning Cycle

In the development programs which you will experience as a high potential, you will take part in a variety of activities which could include role plays, games, case studies, presentations and projects. These give you Concrete Experiences which you are then asked to reflect upon - Reflective Observation. You might be asked to think about what happened, what you noticed and what you tried. When you are then asked about what conclusions you can draw from your experience, you have moved into Abstract Concept where you form theories about how something works and how to improve it. With these theories in mind, you of course want to have another go and test them - Active Experiment. It's a natural cycle of how we learn, and when training is designed around it, the training will flow more naturally, make more sense and deliver its objectives more efficiently.

Learning styles

Onto Kolb's model, Peter Honey and Alan Mumford later mapped four roles; Activist, Pragmatist, Theorist and Reflector.

Activist

Activists need to do something and they learn by experimenting. They need to experience something for themselves and work out how they feel about it, so they make decisions based on their instincts more than on logic. Activists seek hands on experience.

Activists say, "Can I have a go?"

Pragmatist

Pragmatists like to do what works. They like to know what works in the real world. Pragmatists like to find practical applications for ideas.

Pragmatists say, "Does it really work?"

Theorist

Theorists like to observe what's going on and then form a theory or opinion about it. Theorists like evidence, logical explanations, abstract models, facts and figures. They don't like subjectivity.

Theorists say, "How does it work?"

Reflector

Reflectors like to observe and reflect and turn things around from different points of view. They like to use their imagination to solve problems rather than diving in like the activists. They like to take time to ponder and don't rush into decisions until they think that they have covered all the angles.

Reflectors say, "Let me think about it."

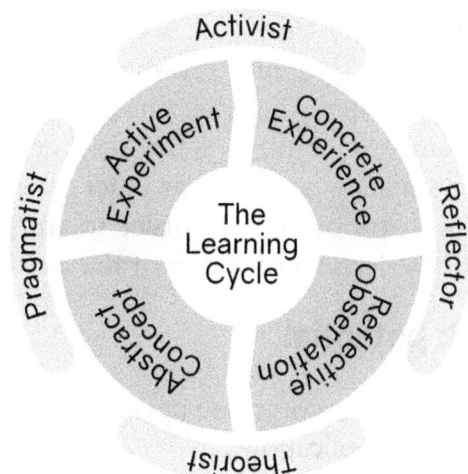

The problem with learning styles is that they are not true. A person isn't one kind of learner, they are all four, in the sequence that is constrained by the laws of physics. You cannot get feedback from an action until you have performed that action.

You might find that you are assigned one of these labels, perhaps as a result of being observed or taking some kind of test, but it is not useful to put people in such boxes and then treat them as if they are only capable of learning in one way. People are not fixed in these roles, they are preferences. In reality, these labels cannot be applied to a person, however they might usefully be applied to a particular behaviour, and that behaviour is often motivated by a person's fears, past experiences and preconceptions.

Activist	"I'll have a go and see what happens"
Pragmatist	"Prove to me that I won't look stupid by telling me that this works for other people"
Theorist	"Prove to me that I won't look stupid by telling me the theory as to why this works"
Reflector	"I feel stupid. I'll just watch"

Studies of brain plasticity show that a realistic time to master a new behaviour is about six months, with daily practice, reflection and integration. It's interesting that the most current work in neuroscience seems to confirm what teachers have said for generations; that students need regular practice over a prolonged period of time with proper rest in order to truly master a new skill. A good night's sleep really is part of the learning process.

Act like a high potential

For you as a student on a corporate development program, all of this has a number of implications.

When you find the learning experience difficult, challenging or tough, the trainer or the training is not the problem, the problem is your own fear. This is not the time to resist or complain, this is the time to develop genuine self awareness and overcome a personal barrier which would otherwise derail your career plans.

When you don't understand what's happening or why you're being asked to do something, do it anyway. Assuming that the training designer is competent, the whole process is designed as an entire experience, separate to its components. If you don't understand one part of the journey, wait until you discover the destination before you jump to conclusions and judgements.

If you don't like the outcome of an assignment, learn to ask better questions about the assessment criteria, preferably before you complete the assignment. The outcome is not a pass or fail result, it is simply feedback to help you move forwards.

If you find yourself being labelled as a certain type of learner, take a moment to consider what behaviours this relates to and what underlying preconceptions or fears might be motivating this behaviour. Get the help of a trusted friend or mentor in identifying the blind spots that can prevent you from seeing what you're doing to get in your own way.

Ask for feedback, as much as you possibly can, and be brave enough to act upon whatever feedback you receive.

Learn to ask more specific questions and you will get better, more actionable answers. Questions such as "What do you think?" or "What would you do?" are almost useless and serve more of a political aim than a practical one. Review the chapter on the second glass ceiling and remember that political moves and affiliations might seem like a good idea when the person you're aligning yourself with is on the way up, but empires have a habit of collapsing suddenly and without warning, taking you down with them.

Where your development program involves live business projects, it is easy to let go of accountability. We have seen too many projects fail simply because the project team failed to make their project a priority until they were so close to the deadline that their rushed meetings and weak planning only made them look even worse than if they had made the decision to not work on the project, because at least then they would haven taken some responsibility for the lack of results. Your career is your future. We have seen the members of disengaged project teams removed from the list of high potentials, and we have also seen project teams generate outstanding, innovative results which led to every member of the team being promoted. If you feel that your team colleagues are not engaged, simply carry on without them. Reduce the project scope so that you can at least achieve something valuable by yourself.

If you want one very simple, actionable piece of advice that will help you to get the most from every development opportunity and at the same time signal that you were an excellent nomination for high potential development then it is this; show up for the sessions, pay attention, throw yourself into the activities and complete the assignments. It's not complicated.

The Future

We have taken a journey together through the minds of leaders and, most importantly, the minds of the people who are making decisions about your leadership future. We live in an age where we are all totally reliant on everything necessary to live and work. There is almost nothing that you can do for yourself. Can you find clean water? Find and prepare your own food? How long would you survive if civilisation were to fall?

Being inter-dependent on each other is a frightening thought only if you believe yourself to be in control of your life. Once you surrender to the fact that you are an inseparable part of a glorious whole, the possibilities becomes as diverse and endless as the myriad facets of human relationships. This simple truth manifests in teachings that are as old as mankind. Do unto others as they would do unto you. If you want to feel good about yourself, serve others. Surround yourself with people who you aspire to be like.

Your success, whatever that means to you, is not up to you for two very important reasons. First, you don't get to define what success actually means. Second, you don't reward yourself. For both the head and tail of success, we are dependent on others.

Your own personal definition of success was set in stone long before you were born. Your ancestors decided what, in your family culture, was desirable and worthy of reward. Was it hard work? Kindness? Luck? Ruthless pursuit of your goals? Wealth? Beauty? Strength? Aggression? Intelligence? Humour?

How was this measure of success influenced by stereotypes of culture and gender? Were you a clever boy or a pretty girl? A tough boy or a submissive girl? A sensitive boy or a girl who was just as good as any boy?

You might never know the answers to these questions, yet if you look around you, at your family, your friends, your career history, you'll see the influence of your ancestors written into every footstep. This might make for uncomfortable viewing, but it is what it is, and you are who, and where, you are.

If we separate the concept of success into two broad camps, you can either be an amazing success at everything your parents valued or you can reject their ideals and be a success by your own definition in spite of their ideals. Both paths lead to the same reality, that you are defined by your attachment to proving your parents either right or wrong. They are essentially the same thing. The really tough thing to do is to define your own path, because this means going where no-one has gone before. When you're walking an uncertain path, it's much safer to follow in someone else's footsteps because at least you know the ground is secure, even if the footsteps don't quite lead in the direction you were intending. If you father was a high flying banker, you know the path to corporate success. You witnessed the long hours, dinner parties, corporate uniform, overhead the conversations, learned how you need to think and sound and act. If this was a natural fit for you and your progress through the corporate world has been effortless, and you're exactly where you always wanted to be, then we are genuinely delighted for you and also rather surprised to find you reading this book.

It's more likely that you're not where you wanted to be. It's more likely that you feel like you followed in someone else's footsteps but you're not sure they were the right ones for you. It's more likely that the harder you work, the more it seems that success is just beyond your reach. It's more likely that your career goals are in sight, but the final few steps are hard to find.

This brings us to the second reason – you don't get to reward yourself. When you take an action that leads to success, you are seeking validation. Someone else sets your KPIs, targets, expectations, organisational culture and career structure. Someone else defines your role, your succession plan, your next steps. Someone else is responsible for assessing your suitability for reward or promotion.

This raises a very important point, that reward and promotion are totally different things which exist for totally different reasons, yet many people confuse the two and treat them as interchangeable. Many people get upset when they deliver a project and don't get promoted. Many people feel aggrieved when they work hard all year and don't become the next VP. Someone else gets promoted who, in your view, isn't as tough, or aggressive, or kind, or pretty as you. It's confusing and demoralising. You can see the pattern, of course. You're applying your own criteria to someone else's decision. You're acting as if your boss should share your family history and value all of the things that are important to you. Your boss has their own history and their own prejudices, regardless of whether that suits you or not.

The paradox which faces you is this; either you reject your boss' preconceptions of success, forge your own path and give up on your career aspirations or you pander to your boss' prejudice, laugh at their jokes, join their golf club and sell your soul in return for a job title and the key to the executive washroom.

We offer you a third path. Stay true to yourself and your ideals and align the way that you communicate and present yourself with the core principles that drive your boss' decision making. To do this, you must go beyond the superficial trappings of success and look deep into your boss' mind. Fortunately for you, just as your path is littered with the remnants of your ancestors' influence as much as yours is. These glaringly obvious clues will only be visible to you once you have let go of your own arrogance and accepted your own judgements.

In other words, you can only see another person's illusion once you become aware of your own. Up to that point, you label them with judgements based on your own prejudice. Their hiring decision was wrong, crazy, stupid or motivated by political power or illicit relationships. It's simply not possible that they made the right decision and you just weren't the right person for the job. Once you accept that they chose exactly the right person for their view of the world, you can become aware of the impact of your own view of the world and you can then choose a different view. Ultimately, you discover that no-one is right or wrong. Right now, you're probably feeling quite self-satisfied that you already know that there is no right and wrong, that everyone has their own opinions. You know it, but you don't act as if you know it. You don't live your life with that knowledge woven into every thread of your being. You only know it if you have to stop and think about it, and you probably only do that when you really have to. It's not your fault, it's entirely natural. As children, we learn to form our own world view and to defend it at all costs from the influence of others. This has served you well right up to the point that your success in life was no longer up to you.

Recognition and promotion are both investments. Recognition, whether it's a financial bonus or a simple 'thank you' is an investment that pays off when you carry on doing the same things, year after a year. You hit your sales target? Great. Let's see you do it again. You delivered your project on time and under budget? Here's another one for you. Recognition which comes in the form of a reward for what you have done keeps you rooted in the past. What you did was great, keep on doing it. If everyone in the company kept doing today what you did well yesterday then your company will soon be out of business, another relic of a bygone age.

Promotion is an investment which pays off in the future. It's riskier than simple recognition. What you did yesterday might not work tomorrow. Your track record might not lead anywhere. You might be incapable of doing anything new. Promotion is a risk for you and it's a risk for your employer.

A promotion is not a reward for what you have done. Sadly, you will often see your contemporaries rewarded with promotions, although such rewards are often a 'poison chalice', a reward which carries a significant cost such as a promotion into a job which is highly undesirable or stressful. In large corporations, it's common to see job titles used as rewards for fake promotions. Congratulations! The good news is that you're now the senior executive global vice president for recycling. The bad news is that you're still the janitor.

Judge your progress, not by the job title you're awarded but by the level of authority that you're given. This can be measured in terms of the number of people in your team or the size of the budget you're responsible for. Forget job titles. When you write your CV, resumé or LinkedIn profile, you can make up any job title you like. Your contemporaries and competitors might be impressed by your job title but a hiring manager only wants to know the facts - the size of your team and your scope of authority. They want hard proof of your past achievements because they fall into the common human trap of thinking that what you did in the past, somewhere else and in different circumstance, you can repeat, on demand, in the future. When you say that you personally spearheaded a major campaign to restructure the corporate resource inventory, you know the truth that you tidied the office stationery cupboard.

What you can see from all of this is that your past, your history, is just a story - one of many possible stories which you can tell. You can be a victim or a hero, a healer or a destroyer of worlds. It's up to you. The story you tell will always be true, from a certain point of view. The trick, as far as your career is concerned, is to align your truth with the values and thought processes of the person making the decision about your next career step.

That career decision maker will take your story and project it forwards in time, just like a gambling addict thinks they see hidden patterns in sports data. The factual aspect of the story itself is largely irrelevant, what matters is how plausible the story sounds and how much intent you demonstrated at each step.

For example, you can say that you were made redundant, that you were forced out in a political restructure or that your employer went out of business, which makes you the victim of the story, waiting passively for events to carry you along, hopefully in a way which benefits you. A story like this is only attractive to a controlling leader who wants to be surrounded by 'yes men'. A story like this signals that you are happy to be pushed around as long as you get to keep your job.

The same events can of course be told as opportunities, where you sought redundancy as an opportunity to seek a new path, where you chose to abandon a job that you loved because the political climate was unpalatable to you or where you loyally supported your ailing employer, standing by your colleagues as you bravely helped them to the lifeboats. You don't have to sound like a superhero, you simply need a reason for the decisions that you made, and those decisions need to be consistent over time. This is the essence of the 'career trajectory' that one executive search consultant told us about. When you have a career trajectory, you are the agent, the pilot, the creator of your destiny. Without, you are merely a passenger, along for the ride.

When you act as if you are in control of your destiny, you create a path which demands success and potentially brings success to those associated with you. Perhaps this is why global football clubs spend so much money on new players; not for their track record but for their intrinsic confidence that success is possible. Perhaps they are not expected to 'save' the club with their goal scoring ability, perhaps they are expected to show the other players a standard to live up to. Being at the top of the league isn't only possible, it has already happened. A compelling belief unifies a team. Success becomes familiar, expected.

When you stand in your current career position and look to the future, what do you see? Do you see only the next step with nothing beyond? Do you see a far off goal, too distant to reach?

Imagine that you could return to the very beginning and look forwards to where you are now. Does the journey seem easier or more difficult than the reality you have lived through? Do you see steps and dead ends which now seem unnecessary? Do you see challenges and risks or merely experiences and decisions? Do you appreciate what you have learned along the way?

When you take the absolute, concrete knowledge that you are where you are right now, having travelled the path behind you, and you place that knowledge way out in the future, carrying forwards the comforting certainty and exciting familiarity, you might finally realise the simplest and most important truth of all – that you really can achieve whatever you put your mind to.

Appendices

Research Methodology

The research approach was delivered in four stages.

The first stage was based on direct observations of talent management programs over the past 15 years. The same phenomenon was observed in all of these, in that regardless of the program design or system used to select participants, a predictable pattern of engagement emerges, ranging from highly engaged to highly disengaged.

For the second stage, interview respondents were drawn from an overall group of around 100 people who have taken part in talent programs over the last 4 years, plus managers in their organisations and external recruiters. 76 leaders were interviewed to understand how they identify 'high potential' future leaders in their teams.

Third stage data was gathered using an online questionnaire which aimed to identify the prevalence of formal talent management programs in today's organisations, along with the typical spend and efficacy. 31 respondents provided data.

From the patterns identified in this first set of qualitative data, the fourth stage was an online questionnaire which was used to collect quantitative data to determine the relevance and impact of findings from the first stage. This questionnaire was promoted through social media networks and contacts, a total of around 3,000 people, and the final sample size was 316.

The aim of this fourth questionnaire was to identify any correlation between the subjective qualities of leadership and the self-perception of leaders making recommendations for 'high potential' talent management program candidates. In short, did the respondents apply any objective criteria to the selection process, and if not, was the process subject to individual bias.

Organisational profiles

A variety of organisations were observed during stage one of this research, including:

- A global defence, mining and aviation contractor based in the UK

- A global specialist in industrial automation based in the USA

- A global, US based manufacturer of products for engineering, entertainment and F&B

- A UK based national specialist retailer/wholesaler

- A UK based national convenience retailer

- A Middle East & Asia based specialist retailer

The interviews for stage 2 were largely carried out within these organisations.

The surveys in stages 3 and 4 were open to any respondents and do not focus on any particular organisation or sector.

Research findings

As previously mentioned, the same phenomenon was observed in a number of talent management programs over the past 15 years, in that regardless of the program design or system used to select participants, a predictable pattern of engagement emerges, ranging from highly engaged to highly disengaged, as illustrated in Appendix 12.1, section 12.1.2. The critical issue is that participation in these programs was largely voluntary, which raises the question of why an employee, identified as a 'high potential' would choose to join a talent management program and then not actively participate in the activities provided.

The contribution of leadership development must be considered within the context of overall talent development, because development cannot only focus on today's leaders, it must also prepare tomorrow's. Stewart (2011), defined 'talent' as "High performers identified as the future leaders (HIPOs)". Leadership development can be seen as an ongoing capacity management activity in line with Garavan's definition (Garavan et al, 2009 and also "the systematic ... development, engagement/retention and deployment of those individuals with high potential" (Tansley, 2007).

Torraco and Swanson observed that strategic HRD is not only about implementing strategy, but also about "shaping future strategy and enabling organisations to take full advantage of emergent business strategies" (Torraco and Swanson, 1995). Talent management could be regarded as part of delivering that future strategy.

Subjective selection

Based on research carried out for this book, the most common method used by organisations for selection of 'high potentials' is on the basis personal recommendations, either from their line managers, or based on the review of a group of operational leaders and HR managers. It has been observed that where psychometric instruments or other similar assessment tools are used, these are positioned as a second stage of the selection process, with the personal recommendations coming first. This seems to be based partly on the feasibility of using such instruments with all staff, and partly on the lack of any meaningful points of reference for the use of such tools in talent selection.

The stage 1 observations suggest that the lack of engagement in the talent development process could be related to ineffective selection methods, and the stage 3 data suggests that many organisations are still relying on subjective selection methods. Whilst this is not necessarily a bad thing, it must be taken in context of the return on investment of talent programs. With the average program spend of around £200,000, it is clearly in the best interests of the organisation to apply these resources to the people who will deliver the best organisational outcomes.

A sequence of subjective errors

The overall sequence of events appears to be as follows: A leader forms an opinion of who to recommend for a talent program based on personal preference and identification of traits that they share with the program candidate (Berscheid and Walster, 1969, Byrne, 1971, Harvey, 1997, Hoffrage, 2004 and Cialdini, 2016).

1. Having formed an opinion about who constitutes a 'high potential', the leaders then defend this opinion, despite any counter-evidence from the person's program engagement or their job KPIs (Festinger et al, 1956, Cialdini, 2016).

2. HR managers who design and organise such programs continue to use subjective selection methods, despite research evidence and their own experience and knowledge of best practice, possibly in order to maintain political relationships with organisational leaders.

3. By focusing on anecdotal evidence and program outcomes for the minority of highly engaged participants, the HR managers imply that the program has been a great success (Wason, 1960).

4. The same individual biases and subjective selection methods then persist for the next talent program.

Lack of control comparisons

In point 4 above, it is also important to note that during none of the programs observed did HR managers conduct any control-group experiments. Where program participants achieved promotions during the time frame of the program, this was causally attributed to the success of the program without considering the possibility that these people, being highly engaged, would have achieved promotions anyway. It seems possible that the program accelerated their promotion due to the 'halo effect' (Thorndike, 1920) of being recognised as a high potential rather than because of significant program contribution to their personal development.

Based on feedback from program participants, there is no doubt that the highly engaged participants enjoyed it immensely and found it valuable, but the point must be considered that what they gained from the program, as valuable as they found it, was not the direct cause of their promotion.

Attractiveness begets leadership

An extract from Wikipedia (2018) is particularly relevant in explaining the connection between attractiveness or familiarity and expectations of a person's leadership capability.

"A study by Verhulst, Lodge & Lavine (2010) found that attractiveness and familiarity are strong predictors of decisions regarding who is put in a position of leadership. Judgments made following one-second exposures to side-by-side photos of two US congressional candidates were reasonably predictive of election outcomes. Attractiveness and familiarity were correlated with competence in this study. Candidates who appeared more attractive and familiar were also seen as more competent and were found more likely to be elected.

Similar studies (Palmer & Peterson 2012) found that even when taking factual knowledge into account, candidates who were rated as more attractive were still perceived as more knowledgeable. These results suggest that the halo effect greatly impacts how individuals perceive political knowledge and it demonstrates the powerful influence of the halo effect in politics."

The data produced by the stage 4 questionnaire seems to confirm the biases discussed here. Whilst this should not be surprising, the important point to observe is the extent to which these issues are prevalent in organisations, even a century after these psychological phenomena were first documented.

Maintaining the status quo

An alternative view would be that the very nature of succession planning presupposes that a leader hands their legacy over to a direct replacement, and the subjective selection methods identified in this research would be an efficient way to achieve that. The selection and development systems discussed here would be an effective way to maintain an organisational 'status quo', which at times of economic and political stability may be appropriate. However, market forces in a capitalist economy will always exert pressure on organisations to innovate and improve, which in turn presupposes ongoing change.

Stage 1 Observations

As previously mentioned, direct observations of talent management program participants over the past 15 years seems to have revealed a consistent pattern of program engagement.

The following bar chart shows the number of participants engaging in coaching sessions over the course of a 12 month talent program.

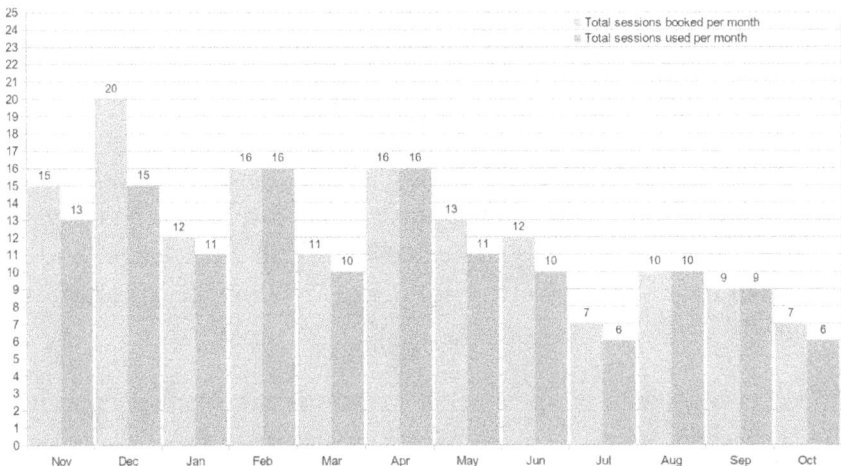

A clear pattern of engagement can be extrapolated from this data, wherein the minimum and maximum chart values correlate with the number of actively engaged participants, and the variation from month to month exactly matches the organisation's quarterly financial reporting periods.

What this raw data demonstrates is that in any month, 7 out of 25 participants (28%) almost never engage, 6 out of 25 participants (24%) almost always engage, and the remaining 10 participants (40%) will engage when they are not under pressure to hit quarterly targets, and their engagement will drop as their priorities shift throughout the quarter. Two participants (8%) left the organisation during the time that the program was running. These figures are typical for all of the programs observed.

Engagement distribution

The following bell curve illustrates the distribution of these three types of talent program participants.

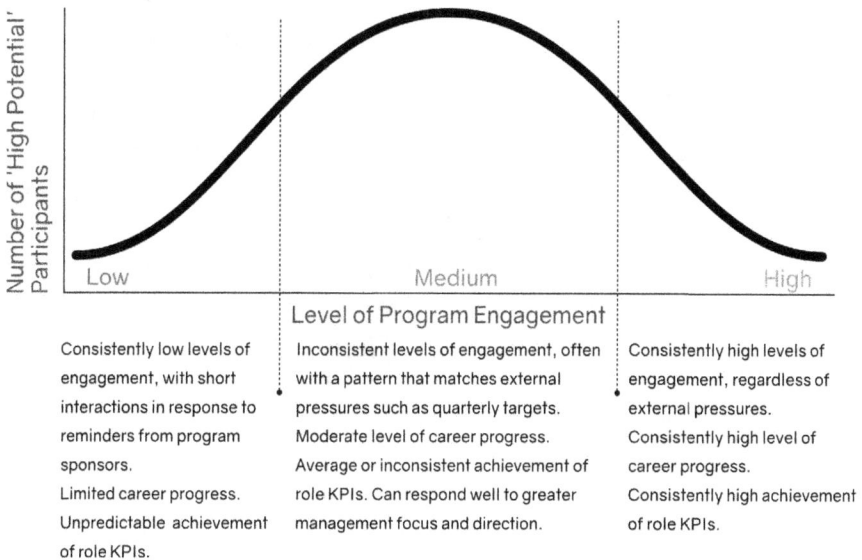

Number of 'High Potential' Participants

Low   Medium   High

Level of Program Engagement

Consistently low levels of engagement, with short interactions in response to reminders from program sponsors. Limited career progress. Unpredictable achievement of role KPIs.	Inconsistent levels of engagement, often with a pattern that matches external pressures such as quarterly targets. Moderate level of career progress. Average or inconsistent achievement of role KPIs. Can respond well to greater management focus and direction.	Consistently high levels of engagement, regardless of external pressures. Consistently high level of career progress. Consistently high achievement of role KPIs.

From these initial observations, it can at least be concluded that not all participants enrolled in a 'hipo' talent management program live up to the expectations of program sponsors.

The top quartile of program participants show consistently high levels of engagement, regardless of external pressures. They achieve high level of achievement of career progress and high level of achievement by role KPIs.

The bottom quartile of program participants show consistently low levels of engagement, perhaps with short interactions in direct response to repeated reminders from program sponsors. They exhibit little career progress and unpredictable level of achievement by role KPIs, even though they are still subjectively identified as 'high potentials'.

Perhaps the most interesting group of participants are those in the midline of program engagement. They demonstrate inconsistent levels of engagement, often with a pattern that matches external pressures such as quarterly targets.

With moderate level of achievement of career progress, they exhibit average levels of achievement by role KPIs, and can respond well to greater management focus and direction.

Talent program observations seem to suggest that with no change to the design of the talent programs, around one quarter of participants will greatly benefit regardless of any other factors because they see the program as an opportunity. These employees would most likely perform will with the right support, even without the talent program, and therefore the incremental value of the program cost must be questioned.

Equally, around one quarter of participants will not benefit from the program, regardless of any other factors, because they choose not to engage in the process.

This leaves a majority of 40% of participants who would seem to offer the greatest Return On Investment, by developing partially engaged employees to higher levels of engagement and performance.

Leaders versus followers

Early leadership theories, founded in the realm of industrial psychology, tended to focus on the characteristics and behaviours of leaders, whereas later theories begin to consider the relevance of followers and the situational nature of leadership (Bolden, R. et al., 2003). Bass (2010) proposes the 'transformational' model of leadership, in which the leader is not just someone with a vision who walks ahead of the group, the leader's primary focus is on their relationship with their team, in which motivation and productivity result from the team's ownership of the task. This contrasts sharply with the old 'command and control' leadership style (Theory X), based on the belief that people do not want to work and must be controlled in order to produce output (McGregor, 1960).

For leadership effectiveness to be relative to the application of skills within an environment or situation, the leader must be able to learn new skills in order to maintain their leadership effectiveness. This points to the conclusion that all leadership skills must be learned, because the leader will continually find themselves in new situations as the business environment evolves.

Situational leadership

Much academic theory supports the situational view. The Managerial Grid Model created by Blake and Mouton (1964) identifies five leadership styles based on the leader's concern for people versus production. Fiedler's (1967) situational contingency theory proposes that group effectiveness depends on the match between a leader's style and the nature of the situation. Hersey-Blanchard Situational Leadership (1977) describes four types of management behaviour, based on two dimensions of an employee's competence and maturity. Tannenbaum and Schmidt (1973) also theorised that the most effective manager could choose the style most appropriate to the situation.

If leadership is an emergent property of a social group (Curral et al, 2016) then leadership qualities are indeed innate, and would emerge naturally in any group situation. Research into engagement and productivity would also support this view (Blomme et al, 2015).

Categories of leadership behaviour

Many leadership models such as Tannenbaum and Schmidt (1973) and Mintzberg (1971) abstract leadership behaviours into more categorical descriptions, such as Mintzberg's 'Figurehead' or 'Negotiator', making it more difficult to correlate the behavioural characteristics from this project's research to those categories, and this in turn presupposes that there are different 'types' of leaders, each with a distinctive set of behaviours. For this research, respondents were not asked to refer to a particular type of leader; only to consider a type of person who they would regard as a leader, independent of context. This would seem closer to Curral's (2016) interpretation as leadership as a property which emerges from the leader-follower relationship, and is not limited to a fixed number of categories.

Stage 2 observations

Interview respondents were drawn from an overall group of around 100 people who have taken part in talent programs over the last 4 years, plus managers in their organisations and external recruiters. 76 leaders were interviewed to understand how they identify 'high potential' future leaders in their teams, and from their responses, a set of characteristics was created, as follows:

- Attention to detail

- Team player, collaborative, builds relationships

- Accountability, integrity

- Alignment, customer focus

- Open, approachable, good listener

- Business knowledge

- Strength, persistence, flexibility

- Delegate, develop your team

- Decisive, analytical

- Passionate

- Focus on goals, KPIs

- Fast to decide and act

- Creative

- Good communication

- Time management, multitasking

- Personal learning

- Cultural adaptation

- Healthy

Whilst all of these characteristics appear to be 'positive', not all of them can be said to be universally accepted leadership traits or behaviours. There must be some degree of subjectivity in this list, and this cannot be regarded as any definitive list of what a person must demonstrate in order to be seen as a leader. What is missing from the majority of these traits is any sense of a relationship with followers, without which a leader has no-one to lead.

Researching the opinions of leaders

Based on discussions with leaders during the first stage of project research, a pattern seemed to emerge within the qualities that a leader looks for when identifying future leaders.

In order to test that pattern, a simple method was built into both the interview and the stage 4 questionnaire as follows.

At the start of the interview, the respondent was asked to list what they saw as the most important qualities of a leader.

The respondent was then asked a number of other questions, some relevant to the study, some not, in order to shift their focus away from the first question.

At the end of the interview, the respondent was asked to list what they saw as the qualities which had enabled them to achieve a leadership position in their career.

In analysing the data, the responses to the first and last questions were compared.

The result of this is that the qualities that a leader looks for when identifying future leaders are the very same qualities that they attribute to themselves.

We like people like us

According to Berscheid and Walster (1969) and Byrne (1971), people are more strongly attracted to others who share similar attitudes, as determined through their interactions and behaviours. People who share similar important attitudes such as home and family are more likely to be attracted to each other than those who share less important attitudes such as preferences for colours or cars.

Sharing similar attitudes suggests that a person is not alone in their beliefs or preferences. If this is the case, then a leader, operating within a high-risk, high-pressure environment would indeed seek out 'like-minded' individuals, particularly as potential successors.

The effect of confirmation bias (Wason, 1960) could reinforce this behaviour, because the biased leader would never suggest someone for promotion who contradicted their attitudes and

Research Methodology

beliefs, thereby proving that their recommendations are always right, when in reality, almost anyone could succeed in the leadership role because the organisational structure around them supports that.

Stage 3 observations

In order to create a context for the potential impact of this research on organisations, a questionnaire was created to find out what types of talent management programs are in use.

31 respondents provided data, showing the following: 35.5% of organisations have a formal talent management program, with the following types of organisations responding: 27.3% SME

18.2% National business

45.5% International or global business 9.1% Public sector

The investment in talent management

This survey further indicated that a typical talent management program spend for an organisation is between £10,000 and £600,000 per year, with the average being just over £200,000. An average of 55% of program participants were said to successfully reach the end of a talent program.

Identifying high potentials

The respondents were asked how high potentials are identified for talent programs, with the following results.

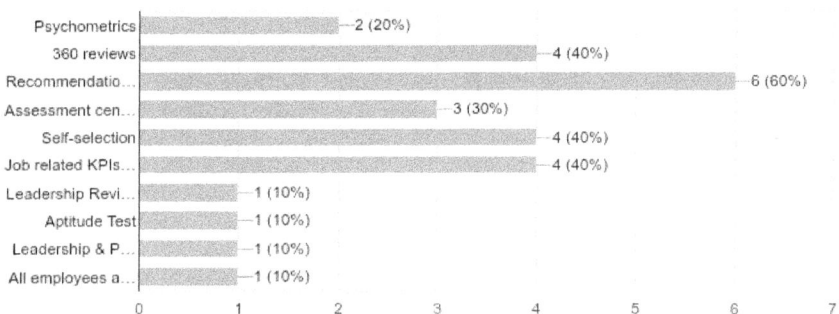

Psychometrics	2 (20%)
360 reviews	4 (40%)
Recommendatio...	6 (60%)
Assessment cen...	3 (30%)
Self-selection	4 (40%)
Job related KPIs...	4 (40%)
Leadership Revi...	1 (10%)
Aptitude Test	1 (10%)
Leadership & P...	1 (10%)
All employees a...	1 (10%)

The most common method of identification was personal recommendations, used by 60% of respondents. The bar chart shown above, displaying the raw data, has some overlap as respondents could choose multiple options, and also add their own options even though suitable options were already there. Taking these points into account, the following pie chart shows the relative popularity of different selection methods.

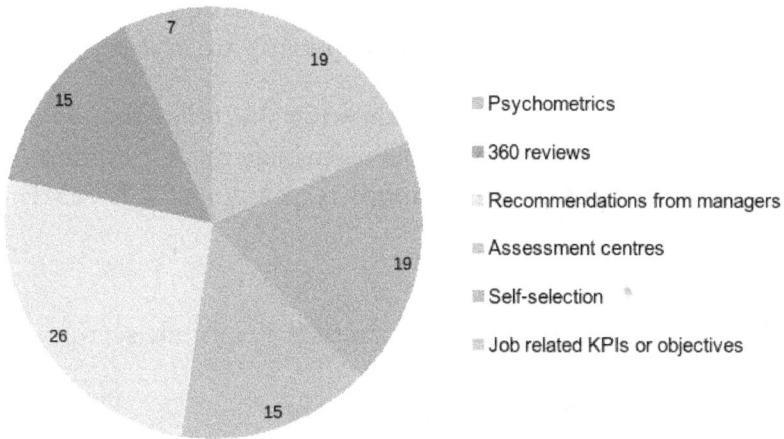

These results could be further grouped as follows:

Objective measures: 41%

Subjective measures: 59%

The prevalence of subjective selection methods introduces a significant risk of bias into the process of identifying high potentials.

Leadership readiness

Finally, the respondents were asked if their organisation assessed the leadership readiness of talent program participants, and 88.9% responded 'yes'. When asked to estimate the percentage of participants who actually progress in their readiness assessment as a result of the talent program, the average of responses was 42.5%. This figure seems to be skewed by one respondent who claimed that 100% of participants advance in their career readiness. If that one response is removed, the average becomes 23%.

Overall summary

What this data suggests is that the majority of organisations do not formally develop a talent pool, and of those that do, the majority use subjective selection methods, and the typical overall program efficacy has considerable room for improvement.

Stage 4 observations

The fourth stage of research was an online questionnaire which was used to collect quantitative data to determine the relevance and impact of findings from the first stage. This questionnaire was promoted through social media networks and contacts, a total of around 3,000 people, and the final sample size was 316.

The respondents represented a cross section of organisational types and locations, as follows:

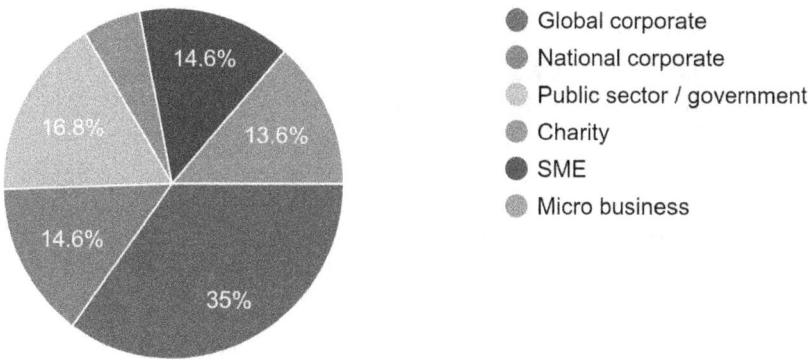

- Global corporate
- National corporate
- Public sector / government
- Charity
- SME
- Micro business

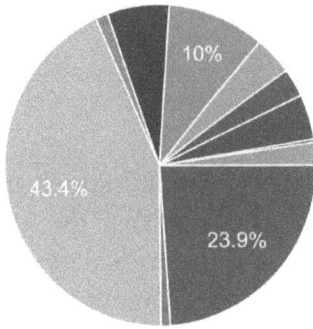

● Western Europe	● Middle East
● Eastern Europe	● Australasia
● North America	● Russia
● South America	● Other
● Africa	
● India	
● China	
● Other Asia	

Leadership team size

81.2% of respondents were directly responsible for a team, with the number of direct reports as follows.

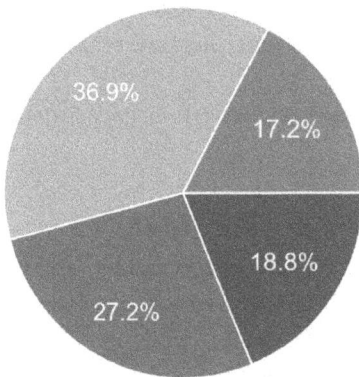

● None	
● 1-3	
● 4-10	
● 11+	

Counting beyond the first level of direct reports in a respondent's team, the total number of staff in a team was as follows.

Research Methodology

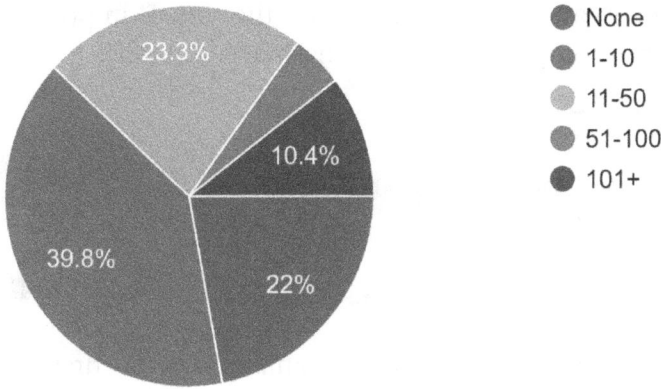

Correlating subjective assessments

The aim of this fourth questionnaire was to identify any correlation between the subjective qualities of leadership and the self-perception of leaders making recommendations for 'high potential' talent management program candidates. In short, did the respondents apply any objective criteria to the selection process, and if not, was the process subject to individual bias?

As with the first stage of research, the interview, respondents were asked two questions, with a number of questions in between to ensure they would not directly relate the first and last questions.

The first and last questions asked were: "Imagine you're selecting a successor for your current role. Look through this list of leadership qualities and rate them in the order of most to least important for your decision." "Thinking back over your own career, what skills have enabled you to reach your current position? Please rate these from most to least important." The data produced from these two questions is complex, because respondents were rating a series of 10 leadership qualities in order of importance. Therefore each bar chart below relates to one of these traits, and the coloured bars within each chart show the relative importance. Whilst this representation does not show the detailed results, it offers an immediate visual comparison that shows two traits as being consistently the most important; 'Builds strong relationships' and 'Personally accountable'.

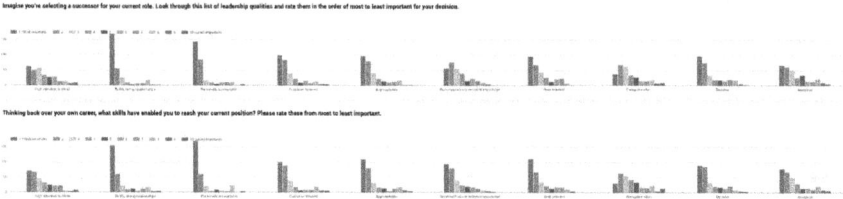

The only leadership quality where the ranking for the first and last questions did not correlate was 'Good business or technical knowledge', and even for this quality, there was only one point of difference in the results. This minor inconsistency could be due to the focus of the organisational culture of different respondents.

This data seems to suggest that there is indeed a direct connection between how a leader perceives themselves and how they make selection decisions for succession planning and talent programs to develop high potentials. Furthermore, when taken in the context of the stage 3 data, it would seem that the majority of organisations are still employing subjective methods of selection, compounding the problem of talent development by stagnating the organisational culture and suppressing diversity in the management hierarchy.

Analysis of the research

The stage 1 observations suggest that the lack of engagement in the talent development process could be related to ineffective selection methods, and the stage 3 data suggests that many organisations are still relying on subjective selection methods. Whilst this is not necessarily a bad thing, it must be taken in context of the return on investment of talent programs. With the average program spend of around £200,000, it is clearly in the best interests of the organisation to apply these resources to the people who will deliver the best organisational outcomes.

In point 4 in section 4.2 above, it is also important to note that during none of the programs observed did HR managers conduct any control-group experiments, and whilst an intentional control group may raise some ethical concerns, the reality is that organisations do not offer leadership development to all employees, and so some comparison may be possible.

The data produced by the stage 4 questionnaire seems to confirm the biases discussed here. Whilst this should not be surprising, the important point to observe is the extent to which these issues are prevalent in organisations, even a century after these psychological phenomena were first documented.

In the tables below, you will find the interview questions and raw responses.

Raw interview data

What is meant by "Leadership Potential" to you?	**Count**	%
Effective communication	23	26%
Ownership	22	25%
Drive growth	19	21%
Acceptance within team	14	16%
Attains results	14	16%
Execution ability	13	15%
Team work	12	13%
Positive approach	10	11%
Business acumen	9	10%
Good decision making	8	9%

Passion	6	7%
Thinks & acts strategically	6	7%
Confidence	3	3%
Continuously learning	2	2%
Creative	2	2%
Emotional intelligence	2	2%
Flexible	2	2%
Innovative	2	2%
Vision	2	2%
Curiosity	1	1%
Discipline	1	1%
Empathy	1	1%
Ethical	1	1%
Proactive	1	1%
Balance of democracy and dictatorship	1	1%

What do you look for as a 'criteria' to recognize leadership talent?	**Count**	%
Effective communication	19	30%
Ownership	16	25%
Execution ability	15	23%

Team work	9	14%
Acceptance within team	8	13%
Attains results	8	13%
Drive growth	8	13%
Good decision making	7	11%
Confidence	5	8%
Passion	5	8%
Business acumen	4	6%
Thinks & acts strategically	4	6%
Emotional intelligence	2	3%
Proactive	2	3%
Continuously learning	1	2%
Flexible	1	2%
Innovative	1	2%
Positive approach	1	2%
Vision	1	2%

What are your 2 biggest strengths & what is the thinking behind that strength?	Count	%
Drive growth	18	23%
Business acumen	16	21%
Acceptance within team	13	17%

Effective communication	13	17%
Execution ability	12	15%
Ownership	12	15%
Team work	12	15%
Attains results	11	14%
Positive approach	8	10%
Flexible	5	6%
Continuously learning	4	5%
Thinks & acts strategically	4	5%
Good decision making	3	4%
Vision	3	4%
Passion	2	3%
Balanced	1	1%
Discipline	1	1%
Emotional intelligence	1	1%
Objective & pragmatic	1	1%

About the Authors

Nitin Thakur

Nitin is a talent consultant based in New Delhi, India, having previously served as Global Head of Training and Development for a US corporation.

A Harvard alumnus with over 20 years of visionary leadership in talent management, leadership development & learning.

As a global head of training & development, Nitin is responsible for defining L&D philosophy, institutionalising learning culture, global L&D processes and strategic learning alliances.

Possessing an in depth understanding of business functions and cross-cultural perspective, Nitin collaborates with business and HR directors to design innovative and sustainable talent acquisition, development and succession management strategies that deliver organisational results.

Nitin works as an executive coach and mentor for high potentials identified for senior leadership roles to accelerate their growth and development.

Peter Freeth

Peter is an author, executive coach and leadership and talent expert, based in the UK.

As an expert in 'modelling' high performers Peter is a pioneer in figuring out the hidden secrets of highest performers and transforming that insight into leadership, management and sales development programs that are perfectly aligned with organisational culture and business strategy.

Over the past 20 years, Peter has worked with business leaders all over the world to develop their management and leadership skills, through long term talent management programs, executive coaching, published books and public training programs, giving him a unique multicultural perspective on the world of work and what makes today's leaders most effective in a complex, 24 hour business environment.

Peter's innovative approach has led to 700% increase in profitability for a leading global engineering company, 25% reduction in graduate development time and cost for a High Street retailer and 200% increase in sales conversion rates for a contact centre operator.

Peter has over 20 years L&D experience across all market sectors and organisational levels; leadership and management development, coaching, NLP, sales, business strategy, and another 20 years corporate experience in technology and sales. Peter is a Chartered Member of the CIPD, a Fellow of the Institute for Learning and Organisational Training, a Fellow of the Learning and Performance Institute, a Practitioner member of the Association for Business Psychology and a Master Trainer of NLP.

Peter's many books are in print in three languages and distributed globally by four publishers.

Find our more about Peter at genius.coach where you can follow him through various social media channels, subscribe to his video channel or get in touch to ask questions or explore opportunities.

References and Bibliography

Antonacopoulou, E. P. (1999) 'Training does not imply learning: the individual perspective', International Journal of Training and Development, Vol.3, No.1: 14–23

Atwater, L. E., Dionne, S. D., Avolio, B., Camobreco, J. F., & Lau, A. W. (1999). A longitudinal study of the leadership development process: Individual differences predicting leader effectiveness. Human Relations, 52(12), 1543-1562.

Ayas, K. and Zeniuk, N. (2001) 'Project-based learning: building communities of reflective practitioners', Management Learning, Vol.32, No.1: 61–76

Bass, B. M., & Riggio, R. E. (2010). The Transformational Model of Leadership. In G. R. Hickman (Ed.), Leading Organizations; Perspectives for a New Era (pp. 76-86). Sage.

Bernard, H. R. (2012). Social research methods: Qualitative and quantitative approaches. Sage.

Berscheid, Ellen, and Elaine H. Walster. 1969. Rewards Others Provide: Similarity. In Interpersonal Attraction, 69-91. Reading, MA: Addison-Wesley.

Blake, Robert and Mouton, Jane (1991). "The Managerial Grid". Houston: Gulf Publishing Company.

Blomme, R, Kodden, B and Beasley-Suffolk, A. Leadership theories and the concept of work engagement: Creating a conceptual framework for management implications and research. Journal of Management & Organization, Available on CJO 2015 doi:10.1017/jmo.2014.71

Bolden, R., Gosling, J., Marturano, A., and Dennison, P. (2003) A review of leadership theory and competency frameworks Centre for Leadership Studies.

Boydell T and Leary M (2003) Identifying Training Needs, CIPD, London
Byrne, Donn. 1971. The Attraction Paradigm. New York: Academic Press.

Campbell, V. and Hirsh, W. 2014. Talent management: a four-step approach. Brighton: Institute for Employment Studies.

Cappelli, P. 2008. Talent on demand: managing talent in an age of uncertainty, Boston: Harvard Business School Press.

Chambers, E., Foulon, M., Handfield-Jones, H., Hankin, S., Michaels III, E. 1998. The war for talent. The McKinsey Quarterly 3, 44–57.

Cialdini, R. B. 2016. Influence science and practice.

Collings, D.G. and Minbaeva, D.B. 2013. Seven myths of global talent management. International Journal of Human Resource Management. Vol 24, No 9, May. Pp1762-1776.

Crosbie, R. (2005) 'Learning the soft skills of leadership', Industrial and Commercial Training, Vol.37, No.1: 45–51

Curral L, Marques-Quinteiro P, Gomes C, Lind PG (2016) Leadership as an Emergent Feature in Social Organizations: Insights from A Laboratory Simulation Experiment. PloS ONE11(12)

Dilts, R, Deering, A and Russell, J. 2002. Alpha Leadership: Tools for Business Leaders Who Want More from Life. Wiley.

Drucker, P F (1999) Knowledge-worker productivity: The biggest challenge. California Management Review, 41

Emery N.J., Clayton N.S. (2008) How to Build a Scrub-Jay that Reads Minds. In: Itakura S., Fujita K. (eds) Origins of the Social Mind. Springer, Tokyo

Fernandez-Araoz, C. 2014. 21st century talent spotting. Harvard Business Review. Vol 92, No 6, June. Pp46, 48-56.

Festinger, L, Riecken, H and Schachter, S 1956. When Prophecy Fails: A Social and Psychological Study of a Modern Group that Predicted the Destruction of the World. University of Minnesota Press.

Fiedler, F. E. (1967) "A Theory of Leadership Effectiveness", New York: McGraw-Hill.

Freeth, P. (2003) "Change Magic", CGW Publishing Freeth, P. (2012) "Genius at Work", CGW Publishing.

Frost, S. and Kalman, D. 2016. Inclusive talent management: how business can thrive in an age of diversity. London: Kogan Page.

Galagan, P. 2015. Trends & tides in talent development. TD Talent Development. Vol 69.10

References and Bibliography

Garavan, T.N., Hogan, C. and Cahir-O'Donnell, A. (2009) Developing Managers and Leaders. Dublin: Gill and Macmillan. Chapter 7, 'Managing talent and succession in organisations'.

Garavan, T.N., Hogan, C. and Cahir-O'Donnell, A. (2009) Developing Managers and Leaders. Dublin: Gill and Macmillan. Chapter 7, 'Managing talent and succession in organisations'.

Harvey, Nigel. 1997. "Confidence in judgment". Trends in Cognitive Sciences. 1 (2)

Hersey, P. and Blanchard, K. H., 1977. "Management of Organizational Behavior: Utilizing Human Resources (3rd ed.)" New Jersey/Prentice Hall

Heskett, Jones, Loveman, Sasser, Schlesinger, 2008. Putting the Service-Profit Chain to Work, Harvard Business Review, July 2008.

Hoffrage, Ulrich. 2004. "Overconfidence". In Pohl, Rüdiger. Cognitive Illusions: a handbook on fallacies and biases in thinking, judgement and memory. Psychology Press.

Iles, P., X. Chuai and D. Preece. 2010. Talent management fashion in HRD: Toward a research agenda. Journal of Human Resource Development International, 10: 125-145.

Janis, Irving L. (1972). Victims of groupthink; a psychological study of foreign-policy decisions and fiascoes. Boston: Houghton, Mifflin. ISBN 0-395-14002-1.

Kirkpatrick, D.L., (1975), Evaluating Training Programs. Alexandria, UA: American Society for Training and Development.

Kotter, J. P. (1987), The Leadership Factor, The Free Press, New York, NY.

Kotter, J. P. (1990). A force for change: How leadership differs from management. Free Press.

Kotter, J. P., (2001), "What leaders really do", Harvard Business Review, Vol. 79 Issue 11

Kotterman, J., (2006), "Leadership vs Management: What's the difference?", Journal for Quality & Participation, Vol. 29 Issue 2

Maxwell, J C (1998) 21 Irrefutable Laws of Leadership. Nashville, Tennese: Thomas Nelson

Mayo, Elton (1945) Social Problems of an Industrial Civilization. Boston: Division of Research, Graduate School of Business Administration, Harvard University.

McCauley, C., Moxley, R. and VanVelsor, E. (1998) The Center for Creative Leadership Handbook of Leadership Development, San Francisco: Jossey-Bass.

McGregor, D., 1960. "The Human Side of Enterprise", McGrawHill Miller Heimann Institute (2013). Available: https://www.prnewswire.com/news-releases/miller-heiman-releases-new-research-findings-in-recognition-of-customer-service-week-227078461.html?

Mintzberg Managerial Work: Analysis from Observation (1971), McGill University. Available: http://pubsonline.informs.org/doi/abs/10.1287/mnsc.18.2.B97 Mintzberg, H. and Waters, J. (1985) Of Strategies, Deliberate and Emergent, Strategic Management Journal vol 6.

Narver J and Slater S, 1993 ,"Market Orientation and Customer Service: the Implications For Business Performance", in E – European Advances in Consumer Research. Association for Consumer Research.

Neubauer, R, Tarlong, A, Wade, M. 2017. Redefining Leadership for a Digital Age. IMD Business School.

Personnel Today. 2007. Boston Consulting Group and European Association for Personnel Management survey reveals talent management tops European challenges list. Available: https://www.personneltoday.com/hr/boston-consulting-group-and-european-association-for-personnel-management-survey-reveals-talent-management-tops-european-challenges-list Last accessed 19th February 2018.

Pruis, E. 2011. The five key principles for talent development. Industrial and Commercial Training, 43:206-216.

Reeves, M and Deimler, M. 2001. Adaptability: The New Competitive Advantage. Available: https://hbr.org/2011/07/adaptability-the-new-competitive-advantage Last accessed 14th February 2018.

Reynolds, M. and Vince, R. (2007) The Handbook of Experiential Learning and Management Education. Oxford: Oxford University Press

Rodgers, h., Frearson, m., Gold, J. and Holden, R. (2003) International Comparator Contexts: The Leading Learning Project. London: Learning and Skill Research Centre

Roper, J. 2015. What we talk about when we talk about talent. Human Resources. June.

Russ-Eft, D., & Preskill, H. (2001). Evaluation in Organizations. New York: Basic Books.

Saunders, M, Lewis, P & Thornhill, A. 'Research Methods for Business Students' Pearson Education 2012.

Scarbrough, H., Swan, J., Laurent, S., Bresnen, M., Edelman, L. F. and Newell, S. (2004) 'Project-based learning and the role of learning boundaries', Organization Studies, Vol.25, No.9: 1579–1600

Smith, B. and Dodds, B. (1993) 'The power of projects in management development', Industrial and Commercial Training, Vol.25, No.10

Steven, A, Dong, Y, and Dresner, M. 2012. "Linkages between customer service, customer satisfaction and performance in the airline industry: Investigation of nonlinearities and moderating effects." Transportation Research Part E: Logistics and Transportation Review, 4

Stewart, J, C 2011, Learning and Talent Development, CIPD.

Suutari, V. and Viitala, R. (2008) 'Management development of senior executives: methods and their effectiveness', Personnel Review, Vol.37, No.4: 375–92

Tannenbaum, R., Schmidt, W, 1973. "How to choose a leadership pattern". Harvard Business Review, May/June 1973.

Tansley, C. et al (2007) Talent: Strategy, Management and Measurement. London. CIPD.

Taylor, S. 2014. Resourcing and talent management. 6th ed. London: Chartered Institute of Personnel and Development.

Thorndike, EL .1920. "A constant error in psychological ratings", Journal of Applied Psychology, 4

Torraco, R. J. & Swanson, R. A. (1995). The strategic roles of human resource development. Human Resource Planning 18 (4).

Training, Top spending trends for training, 2016-2017. Available: https://trainingmag.com/top-spending-trends-training-2016-2017

Turner, P. and Kalman, D. 2014. Make your people before you make your products: using talent management to achieve competitive advantage in global organizations. Chichester: Wiley.

Wason, P. C. (1960). On the failure to eliminate hypotheses in a conceptual task. Quarterly Journal of Experimental Psychology, 12, 129-140.

Wikipedia, Halo effect, 2018. Available: en.wikipedia.org/wiki/Halo_effect
Wilkins, D. 2013. What you need to know about post-recession talent management. Workspan. Vol 56, No 1, January. Pp33-34,36-37.

Wiseman, R. 2007. Quirkology: The Curious Science of Everyday Lives.

www.ingramcontent.com/pod-product-compliance
Lightning Source LLC
Chambersburg PA
CBHW060017210326
41520CB00009B/914